STORY PITCH

SCOTT KING

CONTENTS

Title Page	v
Books by Scott King	vii
Introduction	ix
1. What is a Story	1
2. Character	10
3. Wants	15
4. Conflict	22
5. Stakes	30
6. Genre	39
7. Voice	51
8. Theme	56
9. The Story Pitch	65
10. Using Your Story Pitch	76
11. Fixing Characters	81
12. Outlining	85
13. Blurbs	92
14. What Now?	101
Want More?	103
Note to the Reader	105
About the Author	107

STORY PITCH

This book is a work of non-fiction.

Story Pitch is Published by Majestic Arts

Cover Photos & Design by Scott King

Edited by Clark Chamberlain

Manufactured in the United States of America

Copyright ©2017 Scott King

ISBN: 1548074608

ISBN-13: 978-1548074609

First Edition: June 2017

All rights reserved. No part of this book may be reproduced in any form or by any means without permission in writing from the author, except for the inclusion of brief quotations in a review.

BOOKS BY SCOTT KING

The 5 Day Novel

Finish the Script!

Ameriguns

Resist Them

DAD! A Documentary Graphic Novel

National Cthulhu Eats Spaghetti Day

The Eye of Hastur

Holiday Wars

Holiday Wars Volume 1: The Holiday Spirit

Holiday Wars Volume 2: Winter's Wrath

Holiday Wars Volume 3: Queen's Gambit

Holiday Wars Volume 4: Shadow Taken

Zimmah Chronicles

Cupcakes vs. Brownies

Mermaids vs. Unicorns

Genie vs. Djinn

INTRODUCTION

Word up? I'm Scott King and this is the introduction. That's good 'cause I like introductions. It's where I get to be me and you get to be you. I'll say something odd like, "It only rains hot dogs on the coldest nights of summer," and you decide whether I'm too weird for you to want to keep reading. You should keep reading though, because I have a lot of ninja craft stuff in this book.

What you need to know about me is fairly simple. I find poop jokes funny. I pay off my ridiculous amount of college loans through board game photography and writing. I enjoy teaching and, until we moved to coastal Texas to follow my wife's career, I was a college professor at a four-year university. In life, I want to make a living telling stories that connect and move people. I also want to help people grow. I try to do that with my fiction in the themes and stories I tell, and I try to do that with my non-fiction by offering whatever tips I can to help people improve their craft.

INTRODUCTION

Story Pitch isn't my first book on writing. I have two others: *The 5 day Novel* and *Finish the Script!* The most popular chapter in *Finish the Script!* is about writing an elevator pitch, and one of the most asked about chapters in *The 5 Day Novel* deals with using a pitch as a tool for pre-writing and rewriting. That's how the concept of a Story Pitch was born. I decided to merge what I know about pitching and using pitches as tools, into a system that writers can use to jump-start their stories.

This book is geared toward authors, but because of my screenwriting and comics background, I designed Story Pitch to be useful to anyone who creates fiction. The core of a Story Pitch is about finding the story you want to tell and whether you are writing novels, graphic novels, short stories, screenplays, or whatever, finding your story is important.

Do I expect using a Story Pitch will change your life and help you break into the top 100 on Amazon? No. Spoiler alert: there is no magic code or ingredient to solve all your writer problems. But using a Story Pitch can help make the process a bit easier and, with writing being as hard as it is, why not make it a bit easier on yourself?

The final thing you should know about me is one of my main teaching philosophy: the only wrong way to write is to not write. What works for one person creatively might not work for someone else and no matter what rules people like me tell you to use, the only real rule is that if you want to be a writer you must write. The only right way to write is the way that allows you to write your story. Fingers crossed, a Story Pitch will help you do that.

WHAT IS A STORY

A PITCH IS a description of a story that a person uses to sell it. In Hollywood, it might be that a writer is pitching a screenplay to producers, hoping they buy it. In traditional publishing, it might be an author pitching a novel to an agent who would then pitch it to one of the big six publishers.

Anytime you meet someone and they ask you about what you've written, whether it's a novella, short story, or full-blown three-hundred-thousand-word epic, what you say back to them is a pitch.

Pitching is part of a writer's world. No matter how much you might hate giving one, you can't escape it. Book blurbs that appear on the back of a novel or on a retailer website are also pitches. They are carefully crafted descriptions meant to sell the story to a potential reader.

You can use a Story Pitch to create all the pitches I described above, but the main goal of a Story Pitch isn't to sell the idea of your story to someone else. A Story Pitch is meant to be a tool you can use when pre-writing, writing, and re-writing your story.

Whittled down, a Story Pitch is a synopsis that introduces the key elements of your story, serves as a guide post while writing, and creates enough interest to hook the listener so they'll want more.

Before writing a Story Pitch, you need to understand what story is. Growing up, I was told that story is rising action with a climax followed by falling action. It also has a beginning, middle, and end. (I have no idea why K-12 teachers always emphasize the beginning, middle, and end thing.) In college, I was told that story is made up of character, setting, plot, and theme. And in graduate school, I was told that story is formed from character arcs and character action. Most of what I was taught was a mix of half-truths and bullcrap.

I've found there are four basic building blocks of story.

At its core, story is a character that wants something and the conflict that prevents them from getting what they want. Those are the first three.

For example, if I said:

- Jamie drank the water.

That isn't a story. It is a character taking an action, but without any context that action is meaningless. However, if I said:

- Jamie drank the water, hoping to flush the poison from her mouth.

That's a story. It's utterly simple and not very deep, but it's still a story. You have a character: Jamie. She has a want: getting the poison out of her mouth. And there is conflict: she doesn't know if the water will rinse the poison out.

Let's do one more, but even simpler:

- Mary sat. (Not a story)
- Mary tried to sit. (Story)

A good gut instinct gauge on the two examples above is to ask if either makes you want to know more. In the first, Mary takes the action of sitting, but that's it. There is no want or conflict. In the second we know Mary wants to sit, because she tried to, and we know there is some form of conflict because she tried to sit, but something stopped her from actually sitting. We don't know what stopped her and already that is more interesting than the first sentence.

Although the core essence of a story is about a character wanting something and something else getting in the way of that want, there is one more thing involved. For example, what happens if a character doesn't get the thing they want? That's the stakes.

Remember Jamie? If she doesn't get that poison out, she is going to die! Those are some big stakes. What about Mary? If she doesn't get to sit… we don't know what will happen. In our current example, she has no stakes. So, let's give her some:

- Mary tried to sit, hoping to hide, but the assassin made eye contact with her.

In our fleshed-out sentence we know that Mary wants to sit because she is hoping to hide from the assassin. If she doesn't sit and is unable to hide, I'm guessing things will go very badly for Mary. Assassins are not the kind of people who simply give hugs and walk away. Mary's life is on the line! Those are huge stakes! Of course, stakes don't always have to be life and death, but we'll talk about the various level of stakes later.

These four things—character, want, conflict, and stakes—are the basic building blocks of story. Every movie, novel, or piece of fiction can be broken down into those things. They are exactly what I taught in my other writing books, but for a Story Pitch, there needs to be more. In the tech world, they have a thing called "the minimum viable product" and when built out of those four things that's what a bare bones pitch is. It's still a pitch, but it needs more meat.

To write a Story Pitch you need to consider the other elements that inform story: genre, voice, and theme. Genre deals with the story you're trying to write. In many ways, it is the frame of your story and will impact the choices you make as a writer to meet reader expectations.

Consider the sentence below:

- Hayden flicked the closet light switch several times, but the power didn't kick in.

There is a bit of conflict. Hayden wants light, but the switch isn't working. Beyond that we don't really know what is going on. Knowing the genre of the story would help inform the reader what is happening.

If the story about Hayden was a comedy, chances are the scene would lead into him getting shocked when trying to fix the light or some sort of sitcom situation where he is hiding in the closet while overhearing something he shouldn't.

If Hayden was in a horror story, this would be the part where Hayden found the dead body, or was attacked by some gruesome monster.

If Hayden was on a space ship in a science fiction story, the light not working could imply lots of things, and knowing the story's subgenre would clarify the significance of it not working.

Genre informs the story, which allows the reader to better understand it and lets them form expectations of what is to come. Before starting a writing project, you should know the genre and have a sense of what the subgenres are. As with everything we're talking about, the genre or even subgenres might shift as you write, but knowing them going into the project will help you prepare for the daunting task of completing a first draft.

The next element of story is the writer's view of the story they are telling. Writers have a unique voice and when they write it shows up on the page. Voice is the inventiveness that the author brings to the table. It's their perspective on the world and of the story.

If we go back to the example of Mary:

- Mary tried to sit, hoping to hide, but the assassin made eye contact with her.

If I turned the above sentence into a story it would most likely be a second world fantasy thriller with a bit of comedy. I would probably have the assassin be a love interest for Mary. The whole thing itself would then be commentary on the present-day dating scene. I can see Mary, a low-tiered noble servant accidentally going on a date with an assassin.

That's my take on Mary's story. Yours is probably very different. Maybe you read the sentence above and you didn't picture Mary dating the assassin or maybe you pictured a historical fiction piece or an urban fantasy. As writers, we bring ourselves to the story and our voice informs it.

Theme is the trickiest element to nail. People always get bogged down trying to define theme and sometimes the theme may not be clear and in the open. In a Story Pitch, theme can be summed up by the question, "What is the point of this story?" That might sound like a deep serious question. It can be, but it doesn't need to be.

Looking at our ridiculous examples with Mary and Jamie, let's try to infer some sort of theme from them:

- Jamie drank the water, hoping to flush the poison from her mouth.
- Mary tried to sit, hoping to hide, but the assassin made eye contact with her.

The theme for the first might be that poison is bad and in the second it might be that you shouldn't make an assassin angry. Honestly, at this point neither has a strong theme and that's all right. Your story might not have a strong theme either, but for the sake of being over the top in these examples to make the points clear, let's rewrite both situations to help find the theme.

- Jamie drank the bottled water, hoping to flush the poison from her mouth. She never appreciated how important clean resources were until she moved to Mars.
- Mary tried to sit, hoping to hide, but the assassin made eye contact with her. She should have never broken her own rule of not bringing up politics on a first date.

In the first example with Jamie, we now have a theme touching upon environment and sustainability. The story is also set on Mars. So for all we know at this point, the story might be one in which the earth has already been ruined by pollution and humanity, and now humans are out trying to survive wherever they can.

In the second example with Mary, a reader could pick out several themes. Maybe that one should never date an assassin, or that there are some serious topics a person should never talk about when on the first date?

Theme will appear in your work whether you want it to or not. It's a jerk like that. Even if an author tried to tell a story without theme, theme would still be present. Sometimes that theme might show itself clearly in the first draft, sometimes it might appear several drafts in and sometimes it might be as simple as "drinking poison is bad."

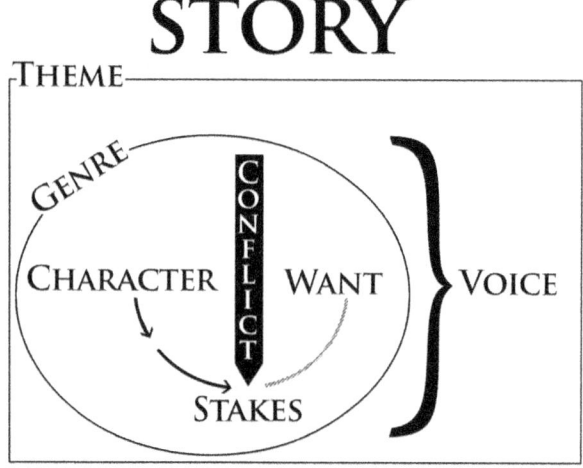

To reiterate, the main elements of story are character, wants, conflict, stakes, genre, voice and theme. To create a Story Pitch, you mush them all together, which we will get to in a few chapters.

Coming from a background of teaching in college, I like when non-fiction books have actionable content. That means nearly every chapter in this book, including this one, will end with an assignment. When in the classroom, students learn just as much from watching their fellow students as they do from creating their own work. So, as I teach you what a Story Pitch is, I plan to create my own and use it to fix my current writing project, *Resist Them*.

ASSIGNMENT:

Have a basic idea of the project you are going to turn into a Story Pitch. I generally recommend doing it for something you've not written yet, but as I'm doing one with my work, you can use something that's partially written or even fully written.

RESIST THEM:

About a month ago I decided to stop writing the novel I was working on. There were a bunch of themes I wanted to write about and deal with and none of them fit into the novel. So, to scratch the itch and get those themes and thoughts out of my head I decided to write a short story.

My plans were for the short story to run maybe 3,000 to 5,000 words. Once done, I'd jump back into writing my novel. That didn't happen. My short story, *Resist Them*, hit about 9,000, and wasn't anywhere near done. At this point I think *Resist Them* is probably a novella that will hit the 30,000 to 40,000 mark, so I'm going to create a Story Pitch for it that will help me figure out the story I want.

CHARACTER

CHARACTER IS the cornerstone of story. It's impossible to have a story without one. Characters are what root the reader, listeners, and viewers into the world you are creating. They are the window and vehicle in which the audience experiences and interacts with the story.

There is a misconception that a character must be likable in order for a reader to make a connection. That is not the case. There are a lot of great movies, television shows, novels, and comics about characters who are unlikable jerks. It's not the likability that matters, it's whether or not the audience feels connected with the character. When a reader cares about a character, even one who is an ass, they will stick with that character through the story.

Characters anchor a reader to a story and without that bond they have no reason to care about the plot. In novels, more so than other mediums, that connection with character is even more important because each character has a specific point of view (POV) to interpret the world in the story.

The lead character in a story can be called a protagonist, hero, anti-hero, or a handful of other terms. For creating a Story Pitch think of them as your main POV character. If you are creating a story with multiple POV characters that carry about equal weight, that's all right. I'll teach you how to handle that later, so for now simply pick one.

Sometimes it is hard to pick who should be your main POV character, especially if you've not written the story yet. The general advice I offer my students is that the POV character is the character they plan to hurt the most. Authors are cruel gods. They beat the crap out of their characters for the sake of a compelling story. In real life, going though trauma and being forced to make hard choices are two of the most powerful ways to reveal a person's true nature. So, it makes sense in storytelling that you'll be meanest to your main POV character.

In addition to being a character you put through the wringer, a POV character should be active. No one wants to read or watch a story about a guy who sits on his couch and does nothing. They want to read a story about someone who is active and trying to make a change in their life. Change is an important part of character and we'll discuss more in theme, but for now let's focus on character.

It isn't always easy to choose who should be your POV character. Sometimes it's a choice you can get horribly wrong. A little over a year ago I was planning a short story and it was kicking my butt. It was an urban horror story set in New Orleans during an alien-monster attack. It had to do with a retired filmmaker who'd once been an acclaimed director back in the day and now served as a mentor to a young boy. The core of the story was about the filmmaker wanting to kill himself, but not doing it because he didn't want the boy to discover his body.

I had several scenes written in the story told from the POV of the boy, but nothing worked and the overall feel of the story was off. Around the same time, I took an online short story class and during that class I shopped it around. The instructor read several scenes and then came back to me saying, "You should really consider telling the story with the filmmaker as your POV character. He is far more interesting."

I had picked the boy as the POV character because I thought it was a YA book, but after talking it out I knew it wasn't a YA story. What really interested me was the internal conflict the filmmaker was having and the only way to bring that out was to make him the POV character. That little change fixed the story.

Picking the right POV character is important, but don't get too worried. One of the best things about doing a Story Pitch is it gives you big warning signs if you've picked the wrong POV character. If I had written a Story Pitch for my story set in New Orleans, I would have saved writing time by seeing early on that I had chosen the wrong POV.

When choosing who should be your POV character, keep in mind the other elements that form a Story Pitch. In addition to being a character that gets hurt and is active, you'll want the POV character to hold a view of the story world that offers insight to the themes you touch upon. You'll also need the character to want something and you'll create a strong force getting in the way of that want. And if that force can stop the character then the reader knows something terrible will happen, because if your POV character has no stakes then why would a reader care?

Although I am starting with character to teach you how to write a Story Pitch, keep in mind that there are several elements that feed into and inform different parts of the process, and you might actually decide to start with theme or even the stakes. Even if you start with character first, the theme, stakes, or voice of your story might change who your main POV character is because the POV character must be the right fit to tell your story.

ASSIGNMENT:

Decide who your main point of view character is. Give the character a name.

RESIST THEM:

Since I had already started my story as a short story, I'm a bit ahead on this one. In my case, my protagonist is a sixty-eight-year-old man named Randdol. I've chosen him because my story is set in a dystopian world and he will repeatedly get the crap beat out of him on both an emotional and physical level.

At this point I'm starting to wonder if I need an additional POV character for *Resist Them*. I'm not one hundred percent sold on the idea yet, but I think from a world-building and conflict standpoint I might need another POV character. Adding an additional POV character is not a choice I should make willy-nilly, so as I construct my Story Pitch I'll directly look to see if I need an additional POV.

3
WANTS

YOUR POV CHARACTER NEEDS A GOAL. In real life, every person has wants and needs and, in writing, you should make sure your characters has them as well. Your character should have specific goals in each scene and the goals should drive the dialogue they speak.

Right now, as I type this, I'm sitting in a hotel in Austin, Texas. Lisa, my wife, is sleeping. I'm really hoping to get this whole chapter finished before she wakes up. I also want to get another coffee, because I'm almost finished with the one that I had stashed in the fridge. I want the weather to stay cool so when Lisa and I go see wildflowers today, we can take our time and relax without dealing with the stupid Texas heat and humidity. I also want to make time to finish reading the new Star Wars book, *Thrawn*, because he is my all-time favorite Star Wars character. There are lots of things I want.

If I froze time, which would be an epic power, and you could see all my inner wants floating above my head, there would be a whole range of them. The bigger and more pressing the want the larger the word is floating over my head.

Having lots of wants isn't a specific thing that only I do. That's how humans work in general. Our brains can have many kinds of wants in a single moment of time. At the same time we have all these wants in the now, we can also want something in the distant future. When looking at your characters, most of their wants are driven by two things: personality and what is happening in the scene.

If you were writing a character and they were sitting in traffic, their most pressing want in that moment would be to arrive at the destination. Fast-forward several hours to around lunchtime and the big want shifts to going to lunch and putting food in the character's belly. That's the nature of wants. They aren't constant. They flow and shift throughout the day.

As the writer, it's your responsibility to be aware of their wants as they change in scenes or dialogue, because their wants will translate into action. Their wants will motivate them to act and say things. Sure, a whole story may be about a character trying to stop an alien invasion, but along the way they'll also try and satisfy a variety of wants.

The only character creation we've done is pick a name. Without knowing them any better it's hard to figure out what their smaller more intimate wants might be, so for the sake of Story Pitch, I want you focused on the big want. What is the one thing they want over the course of your story? This should tie into the core conflict of your story.

Let's look at a bunch of examples from different genres and mediums. I'm going to use a lot of movie examples, but that's simply because it's common ground. I'd love if everyone read the same books and comics as me, but until then I'll keep using popular movies for my examples.

- The Fugitive - Dr. Richard Kimble wants to find his wife's killer.
- The Da Vinci Code - Robert Langdon wants to break the trail of codes and find their meaning.
- The Silence of the Lambs - Clarice Starling wants to stop the Buffalo Bill serial killer.
- The Hobbit - Bilbo Baggins wants to go home.
- Whiplash - Andrew Neiman wants to be the best drummer.

- Groundhog Day - Phil Connors wants to leave boring Punxsutawney, Pennsylvania.
- My Best Friend's Wedding - Julianne Potter wants to romantically be with her long-time best friend.
- Titanic - Rose DeWitt Bukater wants to not marry for money.
- Star Wars: The Force Awakens - Rey wants to find her family.
- Breaking Bad - Walter White wants to provide for his family.
- The Walking Dead - Rick Grimes wants to find and protect his family.
- Moana - Moana wants to save her village and to be a wayfinder.
- Coraline - Coraline wants to escape from The Other World.
- Blade Runner - Rick Deckard wants to hunt down all the advanced Nexus-6 androids.
- Jaws - Martin Brody wants to keep the locals, tourist, and his family safe.
- The King's Speech - Prince Albert, Duke of York, wants to give powerful and strong speeches to his subjects.
- Hamilton - Alexander Hamilton wants a place of power and to prove to everyone how smart he is.
- Bone - The Bone cousins want to escape The Valley and go home to Boneville.

The big want in your Story Pitch is generally what your

POV character will be facing over the course of your story. In a thriller, it can be the action of trying to stop the terrorist. In a horror, it might be to live. In a romance, it might be to earn the love of someone. In a coming-of-age story, it might be something more intimate, like to graduate as valedictorian or to get a dream job.

The three-act structure is a standard for storytelling. It's been used for thousands of years and most novels and movies you've been exposed to use it. When using a three-act structure, Act I builds your world. In it your audience meets the protagonist and is exposed to their flaws. They learn about the world or environment the protagonist lives in and they get to see the kind of relationships your character has with other people.

Act II is the meat of your story. Everything is already set up, which means Act II can focus on creating conflict. This whole section is nothing but the protagonist getting into more and more trouble, all of which in some way is their own fault. It should end with the protagonist at rock bottom.

Act III is where everything comes together. The protagonist rises from their lowest point, learns from their mistakes, and fixes everything. To sum it up like a K-12 teacher: Act I is your beginning, Act II is your middle, and Act III is your end. Generally, the big want that should be included in your Story Pitch is what your POV character is facing at the end of Act II and into Act III. We need to figure out the protagonist's main driving force. What is the one thing they want more than anything else? What one want will push through your whole story?

If you are having trouble coming up with your big want and are only thinking of the more personal wants, that's all right. The smaller more intimate wants generally tie into a theme of a story or a character's arc. If that is the want you know, then simply build your Story Pitch starting from theme.

Moana is a great example of a theme-driven movie where the smaller intimate want is more important than the big want. From an external point, Moana wants to be the hero and save her village. To do this she must take a MacGuffin (plot device), and deliver it to another character. That external big want forms the overall framework of the movie, but the meat of the movie is about Moana trying to find balance between the want of being a wayfinder and the responsibility of wanting to save her people.

In the next chapter, we'll talk more about internal conflict and in a few chapters, we will discuss theme. Since all the parts of a Story Pitch are interconnected and inform each other don't hesitate to jump ahead or around with chapters, if you need to do so.

ASSIGNMENT:

Decide what your POV character's big want is and start thinking about what your POV character's more intimate want might be.

RESIST THEM:

Randdol wants freedom. He lives in a dystopian society and that is his ultimate goal: freedom. Even having written some of the story, I don't know how that want will manifest. I'll deal with it later. He might want to escape and get out into the world. He might want to bring the system down. He might want to kill himself. Those kinds of details are for another time. All I need to know right now is that his big want is that he wants freedom from the society he lives in.

For an intimate want, I'm not sure what to do with Randdol. I know at this point that, for thematic reasons, I don't want him going through a traditional character arc. That makes creating his intimate want a bit harder. My gut instinct says to tie his intimate want with food. Beyond wanting to be free of this horrible dystopian society that is controlling his life, he just wants good food again instead of eating the mush forced on him at mealtime.

CONFLICT

CONFLICT IS the thing that stops your POV character from getting what they want. This usually takes the form of an antagonist, but that isn't always the case. Let's be clear, when I say "antagonist" I don't mean "the bad guy". Sure, the antagonist could be a villain, but an antagonist also can be any force that stops the protagonist from getting what they want. In disaster movies like Armageddon, The Perfect Storm, Dante's Peak, etc., the antagonist is a force of nature rather than a human character. In romantic comedies, there are two protagonists who do double duty, serving as antagonists to each other.

This is why it helps to first decide what your POV character wants before figuring out what the core conflict of your story might be. Knowing what your character wants, you simply have to ask yourself, "What is standing in the way?" Is the conflict emanating from another character? Is it wealth or social status? Is it the environment? Whatever "it" is, it becomes the antagonist of your story.

In school, when conflict is taught it's usually the standard kind like Man vs. Man, Man vs. Self, Man vs. Nature, and all of those. When trying to pinpoint the antagonistic force in your story, don't default to these labels. The labels have more to do with theme than conflict.

Labeling a story like Jaws as Man vs. Nature doesn't do any good, because there is so much more depth in the story. One of the largest conflicts in Jaws isn't between the POV character and the shark, it's between the POV character and the local government. There is also the internal conflict of the POV character being afraid of the ocean. There is the conflict the POV character has with his fellow shark hunters. Notice how there are lots of conflicts in Jaws? In the last chapter, we talked about how characters have lots of wants, so it makes sense there would be lots of little conflicts every time one of those wants isn't met or something stands in the way of them.

Let's use some of the examples from the last chapter and examine what gets in the way of each of the characters:

- The Fugitive - Dr. Richard Kimble wants to find his wife's killer, but he is an escaped convict and a U.S. Marshall is hunting him down, trying to stop him.
- The Da Vinci Code - Robert Langdon wants to break the trail of codes and find their meaning, but the police suspect him of murder and are trying to stop him.

- The Silence of the Lambs - Clarice Starling wants to stop the Buffalo Bill serial killer, but she doesn't know his identity and the only person who does is Hannibal Lecter, a cannibal psychopath, who is more interested in playing games than helping her.
- The Hobbit - Bilbo Baggins wants to go home, but he can't until he helps the dwarves take back the Lonely Mountain from Smaug, a greedy dragon.
- Whiplash - Andrew Neiman wants to be the best drummer, but his instructor is more interested in being cruel and verbally abusive than in teaching.
- Groundhog Day - Phil Connors wants to leave boring Punxsutawney, Pennsylvania, but is trapped in a time loop.
- My Best Friend's Wedding - Julianne Potter wants to romantically be with her long-time best friend, but he is about to marry someone else.
- Titanic - Rose DeWitt Bukater wants to not marry for money, but her mother is forcing her to do so.
- Star Wars: The Force Awakens - Rey wants to find her family, but is forced off the planet where she is wanted by a dark organization known as The First Order.
- Breaking Bad - Walter White wants to provide for his family, but is diagnosed with severe cancer and is not expected to survive.
- The Walking Dead - Rick Grimes wants to find and protect his family, but zombies have overrun Atlanta.

- Moana - Moana wants to be a wayfinder and to save her village, but can't figure out how to balance the two opposing wants.
- Coraline - Coraline wants to escape from The Other World, but Other Mother won't let her leave.
- Blade Runner - Rick Deckard wants to hunt down all the advanced Nexus-6 androids, but the androids are near-perfect humans with super strengths and abilities.
- Jaws - Martin Brody wants to protect the locals, tourists, and his family from a vicious shark, but at every turn the mayor and city council prevent him from doing so.
- The King's Speech - Prince Albert, Duke of York, wants to give powerful and strong speeches to his subjects, but his speech impediment is making it impossible.
- Hamilton - Alexander Hamilton wants a position of power and to prove how smart he is, but his brashness and not coming from a family in power stands in the way.
- Bone - The Bone cousins want to escape The Valley and go home, but the evil Lord of the Locusts stops them from leaving.

There are two kinds of conflict, internal and external. External would be something like the big bad of a story. In Avengers Loki is the big bad, and everything he does causes external conflict for the heroes. Internal conflict is something that happens in a character's head. In Star Wars: A New Hope there is a part where Han Solo abandons the other main characters. What he goes through and experiences in that moment of abandonment is internal conflict, with the result being his return. It's harder to show in films, and when it is shown it's often done through the acting instead of dialogue.

Moana, which we talked about last chapter, is a great example of a movie that handles internal conflict in a clear manner. The whole set-up of the movie is that Moana must defeat a horrible demon named Te Ka to restore the heart of Teffti. The actual movie doesn't play out that way and because it is a musical where characters sing their inner feelings, it's clear early on that Moana has an internal conflict in trying to find a balance between her want of being a wayfinder with the responsibility of being the next chieftain.

Often the internal conflict of a story will tie directly into the theme of a story or into a more intimate want as opposed to the big want. A simple way to create internal conflict is to force a character to make a choice with no good outcome. If you were writing a superhero story, you force the hero to choose between saving their best friend's life or saving the city. The harder the choice is to make, the more internal conflict the POV character will experience.

The same applies to smaller character stories too. Let's say you were writing a story about a high school girl. Her big want is to get into Columbia University. She's hardcore type-A and does a bunch of extracurricular activities like volunteer work and even is taking college courses. Things look like they are going well and it appears as if she'll get into the college of her choice. But when she talks to the recruiter, he points out that she doesn't have enough team-based activities and if she wants to appear more rounded she should join a sport, do drama, or something where she interacts and works more with her peers.

Meanwhile, our POV character's intimate want might be that she's in love with her best friend. The best friend could be male, female, or non-binary. That's not important. The issue is that the only time our POV character gets to spend one-on-one time with the best friend is at the exact same time of drama, field hockey, or whatever activity the recruiter told her to join.

Now the story reaches a place where the POV character must choose between their intimate want and their big want. Do they spend more time with this person they love or do they give it up and do what the recruiter told them to do? We could even ratchet things up. Maybe the friend becomes a love interest, but is going to a different school. Then the POV character will have to decide if they should follow the new love or go to the dream school.

Intimate wants and internal conflict are a lot of fun. They can often destroy your POV character more than anything external, but they are hard to get right. We will talk more about them in theme. For now, I want you to keep an eye on the big picture. What is the big external thing that stops your character from getting what they want? Often the larger and flashier the want the bigger the conflict. The smaller the want the smaller the conflict. The two seem to correlate. Don't ever feel pressured to create a big flashy conflict if the want itself is a much smaller simplistic thing.

Consider the drama of a single parent trying to get a job while dealing with an addiction. They're an alcoholic and so a lot of the conflict will be the weight of responsibilities, bills, parenting, life, or maybe even legal issues. A story about alcoholism is a more character-driven story. It doesn't need a Darth Vader character for the single parent to face off against. So, pay attention and make sure that the extremeness of your conflict is parallel with your POV character's wants.

ASSIGNMENT:

Figure out the core conflict of your story by deciding who or what is externally getting in the way of your character achieving their big want. Also start thinking about what internal conflict might appear in your story, but keep in mind that your story might not have strong internal conflict at this point and if it does it will be theme related.

RESIST THEM:

I know that "the government" is standing in the way of Randdol being free. As written, that is shown as social norms, societal rules, and things of that nature. For the themes that I want to get across it might not be enough. I think this is where I screwed up in trying to write a short story without writing a Story Pitch ahead of time.

My gut is telling me that I need to create another POV

character and that this character should be a cop or solider working for the government and that they are directly trying to stop or capture Randdol.

Deciding to create a second POV character is a huge deal, but without spoiling the story, I can say one-hundred-percent that the climax I want in the story won't pay off or even make sense without having that second POV.

I'm going to name the character Tayes and for now I just need to know she is working for the government and is actively trying to capture Randdol. That is the core conflict of *Resist Them*: Randdol vs. Tayes — set in this putrid dystopian society.

I think Tayes will be my big vehicle for internal conflict. It's obvious that this world is a bad place. Randdol can't have much internal conflict when trying to take it down, escape, or whatever he's going to do. However, I think it might be nice if Tayes, who is working on behalf of the government, has strong reservations about what she is doing.

5
STAKES

THE HARDEST THING TO remember about conflict is it doesn't have to be big and flashy unless your story or characters demand it to be. My light way for explaining stakes is saying that characters have three parts of their lives: their home life, their careers, and their friendships and romantic relationships. The biggest way to raise the stakes and kick a character to the curb is to put all three areas of their lives in jeopardy. When all three are at risk the stakes become very high.

Now that we are talking with a bit more depth, I want to add to that simply explanation. There are two main influences on what raises or lowers the stakes for a character. The first is how much a character wants something, and the second is how bad the consequences are if that character does not get what they want. If both things are high, then the stakes will be high. If only one of them is high, then the stakes will be low.

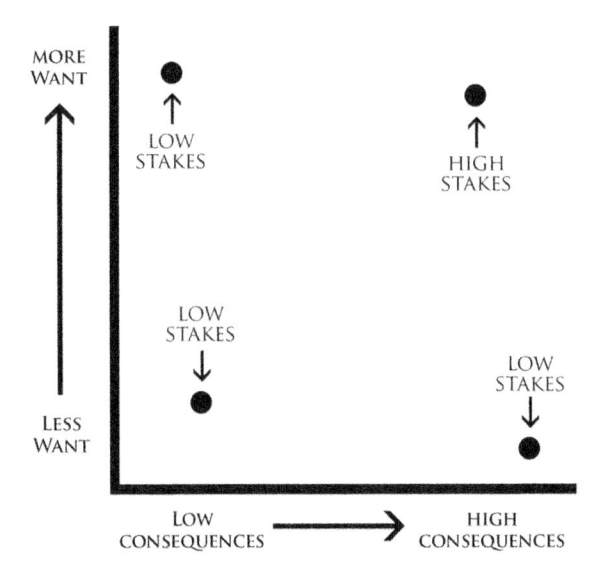

```
         MORE
         WANT    ●              ●
          ↑      ↑              ↑
          |     LOW            HIGH
          |    STAKES         STAKES
          |
          |
          |     LOW
          |    STAKES
          |      ↓             LOW
          |                   STAKES
         LESS    ●              ↓
         WANT                   ●
          |_____→
                 LOW            HIGH
             CONSEQUENCES   CONSEQUENCES
```

As I'm typing this, it's 5:33a.m. And I'm sitting at a hotel in Austin, Texas. I wrote the first draft for the chapter on wants three days ago and today is our last full day here, before heading home to the Houston area. Lisa is once more asleep and I would love to have a cup of coffee. The problem is that I forgot to stash any in the fridge yesterday. The conflict is if I go to get coffee, I'll wake Lisa up. My want for coffee is high, but if I don't get coffee I'm not going to roll over and die. I can wait a few hours until Lisa wakes up and get a coffee then. There is no end-of-the-world consequence for me not getting coffee. Since my want is high and the consequences are low risk, then this overall is a low stake situation. It's not that low stakes are bad. If I were writing a smaller story, a comedy, or even a character piece, a low stakes situation like this could fit into the story. But if I was trying to create high stakes this would be a fail.

Let's add aliens to the situation. Aliens are about to blow up Earth. Not invade. They are lazy aliens and they want to wipe it all out in a single laser blast. They are the main conflict and, because I'm weird, even though aliens are about to destroy Earth, I'd still want a coffee. Knowing there would be nothing I could do to stop aliens from destroying Earth, I would probably wake Lisa up and we'd go to one of our favorite coffee places in Austin like Cuvee or Mozarts. Then we'd kick back and relax, waiting for the world to end.

In this scenario, my want for coffee is still high. However, even though we have added aliens, and Earth is about to blow up, the consequences for me getting a coffee are the same. Earth is not blowing up because I am not getting my coffee. It is blowing up because the aliens are too lazy to invade. So even though this might have seemed like a situation with higher stakes, it really isn't any different from our first example where there were no aliens. Adding in action, death, explosions, and all those flashy things, means nothing if they are not tied directly to the wants of your POV character.

Let's look at some of our examples from previous chapters and decide how serious the stakes are for our characters...

- The Fugitive - Dr. Richard Kimble wants to find his wife's killer, but he is an escaped convict and a U.S. Marshall is hunting him down, trying to stop him. If he fails, his wife's murderer will end up free

without paying any cost and Kimble will end up in jail, framed for the crime.
- The Da Vinci Code - Robert Langdon wants to break the trail of codes and find their meaning, but the police suspect him of murder and are trying to stop him. If he fails, he will be arrested and will never find the answers he is searching for and will most likely spend years in prison for murder.
- The Silence of the Lambs - Clarice Starling wants to stop the Buffalo Bill serial killer, but she doesn't know his identity and the only person who does is Hannibal Lecter, a cannibal psychopath, who is more interested in playing games than helping her. If she fails to stop Buffalo Bill, more women will die.
- The Hobbit - Bilbo Baggins wants to go home, but he can't until he helps the dwarves take back the Lonely Mountain from Smaug, a greedy dragon. If he fails to help the dwarves he could die, but more importantly he will never see Bag End again.
- Whiplash - Andrew Neiman wants to be the best drummer, but his instructor is more interested in being cruel and verbally abusive than in teaching. If Andrew fails, it will prove his family right and he will have wasted his life and amounted to nothing.
- Groundhog Day - Phil Connors wants to leave boring Punxsutawney, Pennsylvania, but is trapped in a time loop. If he fails to break the loop he will be caught for all eternity in Punxsutawney.

- My Best Friend's Wedding - Julianne Potter wants to romantically be with her long-time best friend, but he is about to marry someone else. If she fails she will never get married or be happy.
- Titanic - Rose DeWitt Bukater wants to not marry for money, but her mother is forcing her to do so. If she fails then she will live the rest of her life unfulfilled and empty.
- Star Wars: The Force Awakens - Rey wants to find her family, but is forced off the planet where she is wanted by a dark organization known as The First Order. If she fails to escape from The First Order's pursuit she will never find her family or learn who she really is.
- Breaking Bad - Walter White wants to provide for his family, but is diagnosed with severe cancer and is not expected to survive. If he fails to provide for his family then he will die a failure and leave them in a horrible place.
- The Walking Dead - Rick Grimes wants to find and protect his family, but zombies have overrun Atlanta. If he fails to protect them, they will die and turn into horrible creatures.
- Moana - Moana wants to be a wayfinder and to save her village, but can't figure out how to balance the two opposing wants. If she fails she will either spend her life unfulfilled for not following her dream or feel guilty for following it.
- Coraline - Coraline wants to escape from The

STORY PITCH

Other World, but Other Mother won't let her go. If she fails to escape, then she will never see her parents or home again.
- Blade Runner - Rick Deckard wants to hunt down all the advanced Nexus-6 androids, but the androids are near-perfect humans with super strengths and abilities. If he fails, the Nexus-6 could put all human society at risk.
- Jaws - Martin Brody wants to protect the locals, tourists, and his family from a vicious shark, but at every turn the mayor and city council prevent him from doing so. If he fails then more people, possibly his family, will die.
- The King's Speech - Prince Albert, Duke of York, wants to give powerful and strong speeches to his subjects, but his speech impediment is making it impossible. If he fails then he will be a joke of a king and not taken seriously.
- Hamilton - Alexander Hamilton wants a position of power and to prove how smart he is, but his brashness and not coming from a family in power stands in the way. If he fails, he will be forgotten and everything he has worked toward will have been meaningless.
- Bone - The Bone cousins want to escape The Valley and go home, but the evil Lord of the Locusts stops them from leaving. If they fail to stop the Lord of Locusts, they will never see Boneville again!

My go-to response for how to raise the stakes will still be that you chip away and put the parts of a character's life at risk. However, keep in mind that not all characters have a family, or a love life, or a career.

Not too long ago I was a guest on a podcast and afterwards I chatted with the indie author who interviewed me. She was having a hard time raising the stakes and when I suggested that she try making things bad with the POV character's home life, love life, and career, the author told me that her character didn't have a job.

I told her that wasn't entirely true. The author's story was set in the flapper era and in many ways the POV character was like Rose from Titanic. The character's family was pressuring her into social climbing because their whole life was about achieving a higher social status. She may not have a job as we would normally think of it, but the social climbing was a huge part of what she wanted and a way to raise the stakes would be to put her social status at risk. The consequences of not achieving a higher social status will put her relationship with her family at risk, affect her love life, and crush one of the biggest wants she had been trying to gain through the story.

Let's go back to our example of the aliens who want to blow up Earth. Let's say that the story we are trying to tell is more of a character piece. The aliens are no longer the main conflict in the story. The story isn't about the aliens, it's about how people respond and react to the aliens. It's about how monstrous and chaotic humans can be when they think there are no consequences.

We already know that our character Scott wants coffee.

The big conflict of the story would be about Scott and Lisa confronting and dealing with people freaking out and going crazy because the world is ending. It would be a humanity story and although we could still have lots of action, that action would be grounded as Scott and Lisa made their way to their ideal coffee shop for their final cup of coffee before the world ends. In a smaller story where the focus is more grounded, the consequences of Scott not getting coffee could end up being a high stake, especially if the character arc and theme focus on what happens when Scott doesn't get the coffee. Does he Hulk-out and join the freaking masses? Does he retain his humanity? Does he learn what REALLY matters in life and, in the final seconds before Earth is destroyed, give up his obsession with coffee to focus his attention on Lisa?

To determine high stakes for your story, you need to examine the important parts of your POV character's life. At this stage, since you're not writing yet, you may not know what those things are, but it doesn't hurt to plan now. You should know your POV character's big want and some of their more intimate wants. What would be some high-risk consequences of them not getting those wants?

ASSIGNMENT:

Figure out the stakes for your story. This requires knowing what your POV character really wants and depending on the type of story you are trying to tell, ensuring that the consequences of not getting the want are either high or low.

RESIST THEM:

I lucked-out a bit with *Resist Them* because of the type of story it is. In Resist Them, the government is literally beaming music, messages, and such into people's minds. Death isn't a fear and neither is losing possessions or material objects. The real horror in this world is losing your mind. If Randdol fails he will become a mindless drone with no identity. Those are high stakes and it also tells me that this is a much larger type of story and not a quiet character piece.

6
GENRE

GENRE IS the type of story you are trying to tell. At first glance, most people can tell what type of genre a story fits into. If there are spaceships, then it's science-fiction. If there is magic, it's fantasy. If it is scary and causes the reader's arm hairs to quiver or gives them chills, then it's horror. Yet not all stories are as clean-cut when it comes to genre and sometimes it might be hard to fit a story into one genre or another, especially once the writer starts mashing multiple genres together.

Genre is strange in that it not only informs the story you're writing, but will later impact both the marketing of your story and readers' expectations. Readers are divas. They want you to tell them the exact type of story they expected to read when they bought the book. When the story you tell them isn't the type of story they wanted to hear, your readers' expectations aren't met.

Expectations for story appear in all aspects of our lives. For example, Lisa is a chemical engineer. She does science stuff and the easiest way to explain her job is to compare her to Scotty from Star Trek: The Original Series. On Star Trek, it was Scotty's job to keep the ship running and to stop explosions from happening. That's what Lisa does at the plant where she works. She oversees recipes and if anything goes wrong it's her job to fix the problem and make sure people stay safe.

Last week she came home and I knew right away that she'd had a bad day. I was worried that someone at work had gotten hurt or perhaps that someone directed a belittling or sexist comment at her. Then I thought maybe there was a budget problem, or even that there was some sort of emotional impact to her or the co-workers she cared about. Whatever happened I knew it was very serious because Lisa was slouched and speaking in a low tone.

I asked her, "What happened?"

She lifted her head. She sighed, then spoke in a soft voice saying, "The AC in the office broke. It was down for most of the day and all the chocolate I had in the chocolate drawer of my desk melted."

I laughed, and then I got yelled at for laughing, but the point is that my expectation for the story was off. I had expected Lisa to tell me about a terrible or life-threatening situation at work, which happens more often than it should. But because I was expecting the worst, her story seemed silly. Melted chocolate did not meet my expectation for why she was in such a sad mood. It's not that her mood was invalid. It's not that she didn't have a right to be upset about her wasted chocolate. It's just that from her body language and past history, I expected a different kind of story from her.

Once you start writing your manuscript, you will make promises to the reader through the situations and scenes you set up in the first portion of the story. If your story begins with a huge action sequence, then you are making a promise to the reader that your story is going to be an action story. If you don't deliver any more action after that first scene, you are sending the wrong message. If you set up the wrong expectation, your readers will be unhappy with your story. That's why genre is so important.

The first way genre is defined, when talking about novels, is by reader age. There are five main age groups:

- Children's
- Middle Grade
- Young Adult
- New Adult
- Adult

Children's books are a catch-all for any book below a third-grade reading level. They include board books, picture books, chapter books, and any other kind of book that's specifically written for someone who is eight years old or younger.

Middle Grade books are for readers who are generally in the age range of eight to twelve. The POV characters in these books are usually two years older than the readers and although the themes can touch upon serious problems and the characters can end up in bad situations, the overall tone is usually lighter. The books are generally shorter than adult novels, there is violence but no gore, and you rarely see any romance between the characters. The themes in Middle Grade books often directly relate to the POV character's friends and family.

Young Adult novels are generally for readers who are the age of thirteen to eighteen. The POV characters are usually a year or more older than the readers. The books can be full-length novels, they can have cussing, deal with heavy themes, violence, and sex (although there is sex in this age group, the characters generally have it off screen). The most common themes for YA books deal with teen issues like self-discovery.

New Adult is a genre that sprung up in the last decade and spans the gap between YA and Adult. The POV characters are usually eighteen years old to mid-twenties. There can be lots of cussing, sex, and violence, though none of it is usually gratuitous. Thematically these books deal with characters transitioning into life and having to face real-world responsibilities like paying bills, getting a job, and basic adulting.

The Adult genre is everything else. The characters are usually mid-twenties and up. There is no holding back with sex, violence, or language. The themes can touch upon anything.

Once you know the age of your audience, you can mix and match that with various genres. For example, you could write a Middle Grade fantasy novel, or age up the characters and themes and have it be a Young Adult fantasy novel. Because the content and themes are very different for the various age groups, a Middle Grade fantasy novel would also be very different from a Young Adult fantasy novel.

Keep in mind that the age grouping isn't hard and fast. An author could write a novel for adults told from the POV of a child. At the same time, there are tons of adults who love to read Middle Grade and Young Adult novels. The age groupings are more a guideline for sales and marketing to the right reader.

Once you know the age genre of your story, you can choose a main genre. Unfortunately, there is no master list of genres that everyone uses. The list I have below is a mash-up from Barnes & Noble, Amazon, Kobo, and BISAC (Book Industry Subject and Category). Another problem is that as the popularity of genres shift, a category or sub-category that didn't used to be popular might now be popular and as a result retailers may give it a higher standing to sell more product. To see a current list of genres, check out your favorite retailer to see how they have them grouped.

The two main types of fiction are:

- Literary Fiction
- Genre Fiction

Literary fiction includes books written for their literary merits (meaning the prose descriptions might draw more attention to themselves, and the structures or characters might be less mainstream). Literary novels are held to a higher standard and more likely to win awards. There can be a hoity-toityness to them, which is strange because, although it is a catch-all for anything not genre fiction, there are plenty of genre authors whose fantasy or science-fiction novels are labeled as Literary.

Genre fiction consists of books written for entertainment value and the prose is often invisible and doesn't call attention to itself. Genre fiction books have a more traditional structure and possess tropes that appeal to the readers of that specific genre.

The main types of genre fiction are:

- Science-Fiction - is fiction that deals with the future, technology, alternate histories, or science in general. These types of stories often focus on political or social issues.
- Fantasy - is fiction that has some sort of supernatural or magical element that does not exist in the real world. These stories can take place on Earth or in a fully imagined universe.
- Romance - is fiction that focuses on the romantic relationships between the characters. Traditionally, they have happy endings.
- Mystery/Crime - is fiction where there is some sort of crime or series of crimes the protagonist is trying to solve.
- Historical - is fiction set in the past of the real world.
- Thriller - is fiction that tries to create a feeling of suspense and excitement in the reader.

- Horror - is fiction that tries to create fear or a feeling of dread in the reader.
- Erotica - is fiction that tries to arouse the reader.
- Humor - is fiction that tries to make the reader physically laugh.

Of the main genres, the four I want to highlight are thrillers, horror, erotica, and humor. These four are different from the rest in that each attempts to elicit a physical response from the reader.

In a thriller, you want the reader's heart to beat faster in excitement. In a horror story, you want the reader to be jumpy, scared, and to have actual goosebumps. In erotic fiction, you want to turn the reader on. In humor, you are trying to get the reader to actually laugh. These four genres are powerful on their own but when you mix them with the other main genres a writer can manipulate not only the reader's mind but also their body.

Mashing genres is easy. If a story was about two people in love and having a relationship while on a spaceship, that would be a Science-Fiction Romance. If the story was about two people trapped on a spaceship trying to kill each other that could be a Science-Fiction Thriller or a Science-Fiction Horror. Where things get complicated is when subgenres are added in.

Subgenres shift and change. In the past year LitRPG has broken out, when previously it didn't have a label. So, the list below is merely the best I can achieve at the time of writing this book, but it should be enough for you to narrow down the type of story you're trying to tell.

The main subgenres of fiction are:

- Action & Adventure - a story that has lots of action or makes use of adventure-type settings.
- Alternative History - a story that takes place in a world where one or more events from real history have been changed.
- Alien Invasion - a story where aliens invade.
- Arthurian - stories set in the world and times of King Arthur.
- Christian - a story set in any other genre that also conforms to Christian worldviews and beliefs.
- Coming of Age - a story where the POV character begins or completes a journey from youth to adulthood.
- Contemporary (fantasy, women, etc.) - a story set in the present-day real world.
- Cozy - a mystery story that doesn't get dark or gritty and has a light happy ending.
- Cyberpunk - a science-fiction story that takes place in a gritty urban setting. Characters in these stories often have implants, biotechnology, are hackers, and are trying to take down an oppressive regime.
- Dark (often Dark Fantasy) - a story that has darker more frightening plots and themes.
- Detective – a story where the POV character is a

detective in law enforcement trying to solve a crime.
- Dystopian - a story set in a world or time where the social and political landscape has become dark and twisted. These stories are often set in near-futures and focus on an oppressed society.
- Epic - a story that is long, traditionally more than 100,000 words and deals with a large grand plot.
- Fable – a story with a primary purpose to express a specific theme or point.
- Fairytale – a story that tells or re-imagines a popular fairytale or folklore.
- First Contact - a science-fiction story where humans meet aliens for the first time.
- Financial - a story set in the financial world. These stories often focus on bankers, stock brokers, investors, and people who deal with finance.
- Hard Boiled - a story set in the crime or mystery genre that is dark and gritty. These stories don't shy away from showing realistic sex or violence.
- Hard Science-Fiction - a science-fiction story where science is the focus of the story. The science must not contradict real-world science.
- Interactive - a story where the reader interacts with and impacts how a story evolves or is told.
- Legal - a story where the characters or setting deal with the legal system. These often focus on lawyers or judges.

- LGTB+ - a story that delves into LGBT+ themes or has LGTB+ characters.
- LitRPG - a fantasy story set in both a normal world and a second world. The second world is usually some sort of virtual game, but it doesn't have to be. While in the second world, the character must go on quests and follow strict rules for gaining experience points and unlocking new skills and abilities.
- Magical Realism – originally these were stories set in the real world with elements that seem fantasy based but can be explained through a point of view character's psychology. It has become the catch-all term for stories that are literary fantasy.
- Meta – a story that is self-aware.
- Medical - a story where the characters are typically doctors, nurses, EMTs, or someone who works in the medical field. These types of stories often take place in hospitals or other medical settings.
- Military - a story where the characters are experiencing or preparing to experience some form of war or military operation.
- Myths & Legends – a story focusing on old pantheons of gods, famous folklore, myths, or legends.
- Paranormal - a story set in the real world that focuses on a phenomenon that might one day be explained by science. In contemporary fiction, the genre heavily overlaps with urban fantasy and

focuses on stories that involve phenomena like shifters and vampires.
- Private Investigator - a story where the POV character is a private investigator.
- Post-Apocalyptic - a story set in a world after it has been destroyed by an apocalyptic event.
- Psychological - a story with characters whose psychological state is unstable.
- Satire - a story that uses humor or irony to make a statement on a topic or political issue.
- Second World Fantasy - a fantasy story that takes place on a world other than the real world.
- Space Opera - a story set in a science-fiction setting that focuses on melodrama and the relationship of the characters.
- Spy - a story involving espionage and spies.
- Steampunk - a story with advanced technology, like computers, planes, space ships, and such that is powered by steam technology dating to the Victorian era.
- Superheroes - a story where a character with or without power dons an identity to fight villains and save people.
- Supernatural - a story set in the real world that focuses on a phenomenon that will never be explained by science.
- Suspense - a story that keeps a person on the edge of their seat, waiting for something to happen, but doesn't make them actually jump out of their seat.

- Sword & Sorcery - a fantasy story with a lot of action that usually deals with dungeon crawls and lower stakes than those that would appear in an epic fantasy story.
- Technothrillers - a thriller where an important aspect of the plot deals with technology.
- Time Travel - stories that deal with or focus on traveling through time or dimensions.
- Urban (often Urban Fantasy) - stories set in an urban location.
- Western – stories set in the American Old West focusing on frontier living or adventures.
- Women's Fiction - stories often written by women that focus on a woman's life experience.

ASSIGNMENT:

Decide the age grouping and main genre your story is set in. Then pick two additional genres or subgenres that it fits into.

RESIST THEM:

Resist Them is science-fiction. The story is set in a future and uses technology that we currently don't have. For a subgenre, it's a dystopian and a thriller. I know it is a dystopian because the story is set in a broken world where society has become twisted, and I know it is a thriller because the action, mystery, and pacing will be done in a way to excite the reader and keep them turning pages.

7
VOICE

THE VOICE ELEMENT of a Story Pitch is meant to establish what separates the story you are trying to tell from all the similar stories out there. It is influenced heavily by author voice, but the premise, plot, and everything else that goes into your story also defines it.

If you don't already know, an author's voice is what makes their writing different from everyone else's writing. An author's voice develops over time and the fastest way to find your voice is to read and write a lot. I've talked to both traditionally published and indie authors who are eight or nine books in and are only just discovering their voice. Sometimes an author finds it fast and sometimes they don't.

Story Pitch is written in my natural speaking voice. I could have written it in a more academic formal manner, but I chose not to because I want people reading this book to feel more like we are two writers hanging out at a coffee shop than me being hoity-toity and speaking down to you. I'm not trying to prove anything to anyone. I'm just a writer who likes to teach. I know some stuff and I want to share it. For all those reasons, it makes sense for Story Pitch to be written in my natural voice.

My fiction books have their own voice which is different from my natural speaking voice. That voice is built from my personal taste in character, dialogue, story structure, and all the craft and technical things that go into telling a story. With my background being screenwriting, I tend to write less deep POVs. My normal writing style moves fast so I'm better suited to write a thriller than a literary piece that meanders and is packed with more descriptions.

Since developing your author voice can take years, I don't expect you to know it when forming a Story Pitch. When building your Story Pitch, you just need to know your personal taste when it comes to story. If you are an author who hates epic fantasy then don't write one. If you don't like movies or books with huge twists at the end, then don't add a twist to your own story. Every author brings their own unique point of view to their stories and that point of view is formed from the author's taste.

While sharing the cover for *Resist Them*, I've been asked what makes it different from classic dystopian fiction like *Brave New World*, *1984*, *Fahrenheit 451*, and *The Handmaid's Tale*. It's a silly question because I'm not worried about making sure *Resist Them* is different because my voice and view is defined enough that I inherently know it will be.

A great example of this is *1984*. In 1924, a Russian author named Yevgeny Zamyatin wrote a novel called *We*. It is considered one of the first dystopian novels to ever be published. In 1932, George Orwell wrote a review of *Brave New World* saying it was partially a rip-off of *We,* and then in 1949 Orwell himself wrote his own version of *We* that he called *1984*. So much of *1984* is directly taken from We, but because of Orwell's voice it feels drastically different. *1984* has become the classical standard for what a dystopian is. If Orwell had said, "Well, this is too close to *We,* so I'm not going to write it," then we as readers would be the ones hurting and missing out.

I'm not worried about *Resist Them* being too close to *1984* because I'm not George Orwell. When it comes to story, my taste is different. George Orwell was literally a poet who wrote poetry. As a result, the prose in his fiction flows with a special quality. I know I could never replicate that quality, even if I tried, just as I know that my dystopian won't slog or slush about because I like thrillers and write fast. It will have lots of action, dialogue, and zero poetry.

When figuring out the voice element of your Story Pitch you need to ask yourself what makes your storytelling different because of your taste. I attended a writer meet-up recently and one of the indie authors was talking about epic fantasy novels. She enjoys the genre, but after reading three or four series she saw a pattern where they all seemed to start with a poor outcast or farm boy, that character discovering they have a secret power, learn they are some sort of chosen one, and then they become all-powerful to take out the big bad. To stop this pattern cycle, what are some ways an author could switch up those elements to make a story more unique?

What if instead of a farm boy, the hero is royalty, and instead of having power, they are normal but still have to defeat the big bad? Or maybe the story is set in a different genre. Take the whole thing and instead of having a story like this set in Middle Earth with hobbits, you set it in a school on Earth and end up with Harry Potter or, if you set the story in space, you end up with Star Wars. Don't get bogged down worrying about tropes and clichés. Instead, focus on what you'd do different to keep yourself entertained.

I have a close relative who worked in special education for well over a decade, specifically working with autistic children. She has tried several times to write a novel, and although she has never quite finished one I've seen a constant theme throughout her work with characters who are struggling to fit in because of a physical disability or a mental or emotional disorder. The experience she has from a decade of working with children is a world view I don't have and can't portray in the same way she does. If my relative were to write a farm boy story, I bet thematically, whether she meant to or not, it would have a POV character who was trying to function in a society where they didn't fit in. Her unique view and experience of the world would inform the story she was trying to tell.

Consider what you're offering to the story that makes it different from what is already out there. When constructing your Story Pitch, the voice element should have a bit of you in it. It should be clear what your view is on the story, and because of your personal taste and interest it can make it feel fresh and unique.

ASSIGNMENT:

Decide what is fresh and unique about the story you are about to tell. What makes your take on this character type, arc, structure, conflict, stakes, theme, or genre different from everything that's already out there?

RESIST THEM:

Resist Them is meant to be a dystopian in the style of *1984*. In my world though, I want the government and the big bad to be far scarier. In the first two or three pages of *1984*, the POV character mentions how throughout that world there are TVs which can't be turned off, but can have the volume lowered. It's a great and scary concept, but not dark enough for me.

    I want a bad guy and a government that doesn't let you control the volume. I want a corruption so dark that they don't just have TV broadcasting all the time, but instead broadcast directly into people's heads! Beyond my author's voice, that's how I want Resist Them to separate itself. It will have bad guys that are far more corrupt and twisted and it will leave the citizens of the world even more confused about what is real and not real.

8
THEME

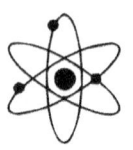

THEME IS A TRICKY BUGGER, but if you think of it as a spectrum it's much easier to digest. On one end the theme is quiet and subtle, and on the other end it's in your face. But no matter where your story falls onto the spectrum your story will have theme. There is no way to escape it. We're human and we want to find meaning in everything, including books.

THEME SPECTRUM

MINIMAL THEME — LIGHT THEME — HEAVY THEME — PROPOGANDA

George Orwell's *Animal Farm* is an example of a story with heavy thematic elements. The whole story is an allegory of how Joseph Stalin came into power in Russia. It was clearly written to get a specific point of view across. Similarly, Aesop's fables are heavy with morality and meaning. Both *Animal Farm* and Aesop's fables would fall on the propaganda side of the theme spectrum.

On the opposite end of the spectrum you could have something like the movie *Die Hard*. It's a classic action movie from the 80's. It's a popcorn film that audiences love for the excitement and sense of escapism, yet even *Die Hard* has clear themes. Bruce Willis' character is having marital troubles so some of the themes we see tie into family values, what it means to be a good spouse, as well as basic society norms like stealing is wrong. The heaviest themes in the movie deal with greed and anti-capitalism, bigger topics that one wouldn't expect to appear in a mainstream popcorn film.

Let's pretend that you are so anti-theme that you have decided to write a story without any theme. You could spend the rest of your life trying to create a story with no overt theme or message, but unless you are writing a technical document instead of a story, it's impossible. It's important to recognize that theme arises from the work whether you intend it to be there or not. Let's hypothetically say that you could magically construct a story that is literally without theme. By doing so the theme of your story would be to have no theme, which means it would have a theme.

Sometimes a theme is simple, like "good will conquer evil". Or the dark side of the same coin, "evil will conquer good". Sometimes theme touches upon serious topics like abortion, gun violence, and all the subjects you should never talk about with an assassin on a first date. How deep or powerful a theme is, depends on you, the author. You must decide. It's a thin line to walk because it's easy to go from touching upon a subject to having the theme feel heavy handed, or like complete propaganda, and outweigh the story.

Of all the pieces that will form your Story Pitch, theme is the most fluid. From the very start you may know what theme you want to delve into but other times you may not discover it until you're wrapping up your first draft or completing the rewrite.

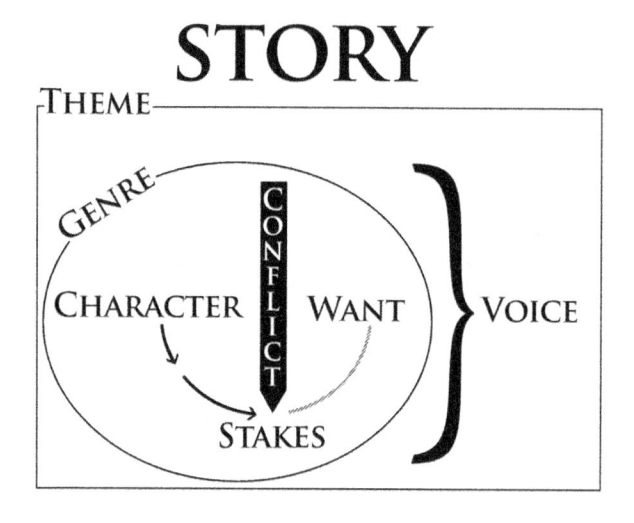

STORY

THEME — GENRE — CHARACTER — CONFLICT — WANT — STAKES } VOICE

In most cases, theme will be built directly from your characters, what they want, the conflict, and the stakes. However, theme, being tricky, can also be impacted by your genre choice or your author voice. It will come through in the dialogue, the actions your characters take, the contrast of different points of view, and even the narrative prose you use to describe what is happening.

With so many ways for theme to rear its head, the easiest way to control it and make it clear for your reader is to tie theme to a character's arc. For those who might not know, a

STORY PITCH

character arc is the change a character goes through from the start of your story till the end of your story. For example, if your character starts at point A and by the end of the story they are at point B (or Z, or basically anywhere else but A), that change in them is a character arc.

The common character arc is having a person with a flaw. That flaw can be something like being an alcoholic, being a liar, being selfish, having low self-esteem, or whatever their constant downfall is. Then, as the story progresses, that character becomes aware of their flaw, learns from it, and overcomes it. One of my go-to examples for this is Jim Carrey's *Liar Liar*. At the start of the movie, it's established that Carrey's character is a horrible liar. It is ruining his career, his love life, and being a father. He eventually is cursed and is unable to lie. Hijinks happen and eventually he screws everything up. At rock bottom, he realizes the errors of his ways and spends the last act of the movie telling the truth to fix his broken life.

The change that Jim Carrey's character went through when going from a liar to a truth speaker is a character arc. In it he learned lying is wrong, and that's the core theme of the movie. The character arc and the theme are tied together.

Lots of stories make use of this easy way to incorporate theme, but keep in mind that this isn't the only way, and not all stories have just one theme. Not all characters learn lessons in stories and sometimes the whole point of the movie is the character failing to learn their lesson.

An example would be the movie *The Godfather*. In it, Michael Corleone wants to get away from the family business of being the mafia. He wants out. He fails to do so and by the end of the movie he becomes The Godfather, leader of the mafia. Michael's arc isn't him growing to become a better person, it is him failing to do so. His arc, although negative, is still an arc. Emotionally and mentally he started the story at one place and by the end of the story he was somewhere else. The character wanted change and failed to do it. This drastically informs the theme. Instead of a life lesson or moment of Zen, the story shows humanity's weakness and the ease of corruption.

In addition to the traditional arcs and downward arcs, you can also have POV characters that inspire change in others. This doesn't happen so much in movies because of how tightly they adhere to structure, but it happens all the time in television or in long-running novel series. The Pendergast thrillers, the Jack Reacher series, the Clive Cussler books, the Stephanie Plum series, and even The Dresden Files are examples where the POV character might grow or change in a single book, or they might have an arc that spans many books, or they might simply cause others to have arcs of their own.

If character arcs are something you want to avoid, or don't want to tie theme to, then you must pay extra attention to all the other elements in your story and make sure the points you're trying to express are clear.

Let's take a look at some of the themes that appear in *The Hobbit*. In this case I'm going to talk more about the book than the movies.

One of the main themes in *The Hobbit* is how extreme circumstances can transform a regular person into a hero. This is shown clearly through Bilbo's character arc from the very start of the story, when he wants to be left alone, till the very end, when he has become a true hero. But it isn't the only theme in the story.

The Hobbit touches upon racism and you see this in how each of the different races (hobbits, humans, dwarves, elves, and goblins) treat each other. Many of them feel their race is superior. The theme is in no way tied to a character arc, but instead comes through in the interaction between certain characters.

There is also a strong pro-environmentalism theme in *The Hobbit*. The "good" races are seen as being in harmony with the world and nature while the "bad" races are destructive and abuse nature for their own benefit. Most likely this is a nod to the industrial age, which was in full bloom when J. R. R. Tolkien wrote *The Hobbit*.

There is also the issue of power corrupting. This can be seen most clearly with Bilbo and the one ring, and Gollum's weird obsession with it. There are themes dealing with revenge as the dwarves try to take back their home. There are class issues showing the hierarchy of rulers and how they treat their subjects. There are morality issues of wrong and right. The story touches upon theft and dozens of other themes.

I hope it's clear now that everything a writer puts in their story can add to themes, even if they don't intend it to. As an author, you will have to figure out how in-the-face you want your themes to be. Recently in my own writing I've been embracing themes more and more. I've tried to make my own stories more poignant and the themes more intentional, but at the same time not push away readers. I've also done my best to put the story first and have the themes reveal themselves as more of an underlying aspect.

If you go into writing your story knowing which theme is important to you, make sure that if it's a more controversial issue you balance it out. You can do this by offering multiple viewpoints from people on all sides of the debate. Most people can agree that murder is wrong. You don't really need to offer multiple views of whether people should murder each other or not, however if you were touching on a hot topic like abortion, you probably need to show characters with different viewpoints and how they might be affected by the topic.

Let's pretend that in the future caffeine is a very illegal high-class drug. As someone who loves coffee, I would of course write a story where the overall theme is I'll be darned if the government is going to tell me that I can't drink coffee because it's my body and my choice. However, that is just one viewpoint. To really do a theme like this justice I would need to show characters who are anti-coffee. I would need to show doctors' views on the subject, the enforcement of the anti-caffeine law, the underground coffee market, illegal coffee dealers, and the consequences (both positive and negative) of coffee being illegal.

It takes a delicate touch to weave theme in such a manner and it gets even more complicated when a writer tries to weave in multiple themes. Lets take another look at *Moana*.

Moana touches upon empowerment, responsibly of growing up, following one's dreams versus balancing responsibilities, how a person sees themselves, figuring out who you are, and those are just the few themes I'm pulling out off the top of my head.

Over the course of the movie, Moana figures out who she is. She spends the entire time trying to balance out her own wants and desire to explore over the weight of being the next chieftain. Meanwhile the character of Maui desperately wants to be loved because, as powerful as he is, he is insecure and feels unsatisfied.

The themes in *Moana* are revealed in the character wants, the things that get in their way, and the actions they take to overcome the obstacles. In doing this the theme fills and informs every scene.

Theme is muddy. There is never a right answer to how to handle it, but there is an answer that works best for you. At this stage in the game, to make sure you properly utilize the tool that theme is, you need to start thinking about what things you might want to touch upon in your story. You need to figure out why the story you're trying to tell is worth telling and what point, if any, you're trying to get across.

ASSIGNMENT:

There is no real right or wrong with where you place your story on the theme spectrum, but you must decide where it should fall. If you want your story to have a clear upfront theme, then it falls higher on the spectrum. You also need to consider which topics you want to touch upon and how you will express that theme. Will the theme reveal itself through a character arc or in some other manner?

RESIST THEM:

Resist Them was born out of me wanting to say something. Theme is very important for the story and, because I have a bit of a surprise at the end, I don't want Randdol to go through a traditional character arc. There will be a small one as he goes through the transition of awareness and realization of the world around him, but it's not a life-lesson kind of arc. That means many of my themes will have to reveal themselves in other ways.

One of the big themes I want to touch upon is Fake News and what happens in a society where there is no media that can be trusted. I could tie that to a character arc, but because I'm writing a dystopian thriller it makes sense to have that reveal itself through the world building and the social rules of the society.

9
THE STORY PITCH

It is finally time to put it all together! You now know all the elements of what will go into your Story Pitch. Now all you have to do is write it. The starting template I suggest using goes something like this:

> "A character desperately wants a thing but this other thing is getting in their way. If they fail to get the thing that they want then something bad will happen."

The pitch template covers everything within the circle of the story paradigm. It's a good place to start and makes it easy to build outward, eventually moving on to genre, voice, and theme.

STORY

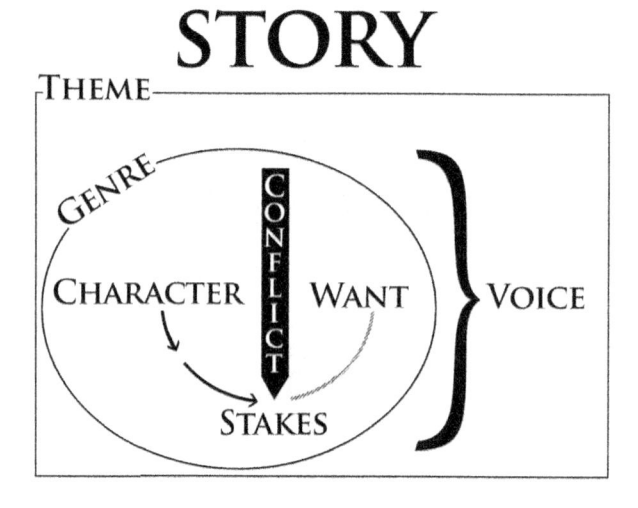

[Diagram: A box labeled THEME at the top contains an oval. Inside the oval: GENRE curves along the top-left edge; CHARACTER and WANT are connected by CONFLICT (vertical) leading down to STAKES. A brace on the right points to VOICE.]

If you know your POV character will have a positive or negative arc, or more details about their intimate want or internal conflict, hold onto them as we'll include them later.

To get started, first gather all the information you need. This includes:

- POV Character
- POV's Big Want
- Core Conflict
- The Stakes
- The Genre
- Voice
- Main Theme
- POV's Intimate Want
- POV's Character Arc
- POV's Internal Conflict

Looking at all the elements, here is what I have for *Resist Them*:

- POV Character - Randdol
- POV's Big Want - To be free from the dystopian society.
- Core Conflict - Is being hunted by an elite soldier.
- The Stakes - If he fails to get free he will lose his mind and free will.
- The Genre - Science Fiction, Dystopian, Thriller
- Voice - Dystopian world is extra dark and can broadcast directly into people's heads.
- Main Theme - Touch upon fake news not knowing what is real or not.
- POV's Intimate Want - Randdol wants good food.
- POV's Character Arc - Learns truth of the society.
- POV's Internal Conflict - Must choose to resist or not resist.

Depending on how deep you got with your planning, or what the theme of your story is, you may not have an intimate want, character arc, or the internal conflict planned out. That's all right. Those three are all theme related and don't have to be included in a Story Pitch, but if you know them make sure you do include them.

Once you have the elements of your Story Pitch it is time to throw them together in a sentence or two:

Randdol wants to escape from The Word, but an elite

soldier is hunting him down and trying to keep him from freeing himself. If he fails to escape, he risks losing his mind and becoming a total drone without any self-identity.

Most of the elements are there but it's still crazy vague and doesn't sound interesting at all. So, let me take what I wrote and build upon it. The pitch is missing several key elements. To make it easier, I'm going to add them in slowly so that I can focus and make sure each is included. The biggest thing I see missing is clarification that this is a dystopian novel and that the world isn't showing its dark nature.

Attempt two:

In a near future, where the government broadcasts directly into its citizen's minds, Randdol Mupt learns that the line between real and reality isn't as clear cut as he thought. While being hunted by an elite soldier he has a choice to make, and the wrong move could result not only in his death but the loss of his mind.

This version is a bit better. Because it's so easy for this story to sound like a generic dystopian I'm front loading the Story Pitch with the voice element to really make sure it distinguishes itself from the start.

The character, stakes, conflict, theme, genre, and voice are all there, but the want and stakes are a bit wishy washy. I'm going to try and punch up the want and stakes with this next version:

In a near future, where the government broadcasts directly into its citizen's mind, Randdol Mupt learns the truth of it all and decides if he doesn't try to free himself then he will risk becoming a mindless drone with no sense of self or memory of who he is.

This is better, but now I've lost the antagonistic force causing the conflict. As you can see, writing like this isn't easy and every time you take a pass at writing your Story Pitch you may lose as much as you gain.

Next attempt:

In a near future, where the government broadcasts directly into its citizen's mind, Randdol Mupt learns the truths that the government doesn't want him to know. Now being hunted by an elite soldier, Randdol must free himself from enslavement or risk becoming a drone with no sense of self or memory of who he is.

For a rough Story Pitch, that sounds like it will work, but just to be sure I need to reverse engineer all the important elements.

Here it goes:

- Voice - "In a near future, where the government broadcasts directly into its citizen's mind…"
- POV Character - "Randdol Mupt learns…"
- Core Conflict - "…hunted by an elite solider…"

- The Stakes - "…risk becoming a drone with no sense of self…"
- POV's Big Want - "Randdol must free himself…"
- Main Theme - "…government broadcasts directly into…" and "learns the truths that the government…"
- The Genre - "…a near future" and "…government broadcasts directly into…"
- POV's Intimate Want - None
- POV's Character Arc - "Randdol learns the truths…"
- POV's Internal Conflict - None

Just about everything is there this time. I'm only missing the intimate want and the internal conflict so I'll take one final crack at creating this Story Pitch:

> In a near future, where the government broadcasts directly into its citizen's mind, Randdol Mupt is merely a man who wants to enjoy food that's not mush. Upon accidentally learning the truths that the government doesn't want its people to know, he chooses to resist. Now being hunted by an elite soldier, Randdol must free himself from enslavement or risk becoming a drone with no sense of self or memory of who he is.

That's a pretty solid base for a Story Pitch. All the elements are there. The character is clear. Their journey becomes self-evident. I'm excited by the theme. This is a story that I want to write!

My Story Pitch for *Resist Them* could be better written, but it would be more of a copywriting effort than a creative one. As a craft guy, what matters to me at this point is the story, so for now I won't spend the time to wordsmith this into marketing material. If you're not aware of what copywriting is let me give you my short answer: Copywriting is writing with the sole intent of influencing the reader into taking an action, usually to buy a product.

We'll spend time on copywriting when we talk about using a Story Pitch for creating a book blurb, but you don't have to worry about making your Story Pitch pretty. The Story Pitch isn't being used to sell your story to a studio exec. You aren't using it to get an agent. There is no need for you to spend hours making sure every word in your Story Pitch is perfect and fancy. A Story Pitch is a writing tool. No one else but you are meant to see it.

Is the final version of the Story Pitch that I wrote for *Resist Them* beautiful? Heck no. But if it weren't for me writing this book and using it as an example, no one, but myself, not even my editor would have gotten to see it. That's important because there is a bit of pride on the line when an author shares their work with others. Your ego automatically gets worried and is sensitive to what other people might think. One of the freedoms of using a Story Pitch is that you don't have that weight sitting on your shoulders. There is no pressure other than to make sure your pitch includes all the elements it needs to.

Just like with mine, your Story Pitch should be no more than a paragraph long. To include everything, it will generally end up taking three sentences, though depending on your writing style and voice it might take as few as two or as many as four. When done, make sure not only that it has all the elements it needs, but also that it excites you. You should be able to ask yourself, "Is this the story I want to write?" and know the answer instantly.

STEPS FOR WRITING A STORY PITCH:

- List your answers for all the elements of story.
- Plug your core elements into the pitch template.
- Make sure the genre of your story is clear in the pitch.
- Add the voice element and don't hesitate to add new sentences.
- Make sure the theme of your story is hinted upon in the pitch.
- If the theme is unclear, consider tying a character's arc, internal conflict, or more intimate wants into the Story Pitch.
- Check for missing elements and if there are some, add them.
- Rewrite until you are happy with the result.

ASSIGNMENT:

Write the Story Pitch for your story. Don't be shy about writing multiple versions or taking the time to weave in all the elements, but make sure that all the elements are there and that each means and represents what you want it to. Once you have a finished the draft, sit on it a day and then come back and make sure it still excites you.

Writing your first Story Pitch might feel a little overwhelming. With that in mind, I've created a worksheet that you can print out and use. It will guide you through each step. To get it, simply join my mailing list and you'll get instant access to the PDF.

GET IT HERE:
http://www.scottking.info/blog/story-pitch-worksheet/

BONUS STORY PITCH:

Since you got to watch me write the Story Pitch for *Resist Them* in this chapter, I decided to write a second Story Pitch, but for *Groundhog Day*:

- POV Character - Phil Connors a Pittsburgh weather anchor.
- POV's Big Want - Wants to leave Punxsutawney, PA.
- Core Conflict - Caught in a time loop.

- The Stakes - If he doesn't escape he will be caught for all eternity in an endless time loop.
- The Genre - Comedy, Science Fiction, Time Travel.
- Voice - Being stuck in a time loop is not a mainstream well-known trope and has only appeared in a few smaller science-fiction stories. In the cases where it has appeared, none have used it in a comedy and a vehicle for character growth.
- Main Theme - Don't be a jerk or selfish.
- POV's Intimate Want - Wants bigger better things in life than his rinky-dink job.
- POV's Character Arc - Changes from being an arrogant selfish jerk to someone who goes out of his way and sincerely wants to help others.
- POV's Internal Conflict - Must cope and deal with the reality that he may never be able to escape from the time loop.

Plugging the info into the template I get:

Weatherman Phil Connors desperately wants to leave Punxsutawney, PA, but ends up caught in an endless time loop. If he fails to escape the temporal distortion he could spend all eternity reliving the same day over and over again.

The genre and voice are already built into the conflict and stakes, so that means I can jump right into bringing out the theme:

> Arrogant weatherman Phil Connors is pissed about having to spend another Groundhog Day in Punxsutawney, PA. All he wants is for the day to end, but thanks to a cruel quirk of the fates, he is caught in an endless time loop. Forced to face a reality where he might end up spending all of eternity reliving the same day over and over again, Phil has to choose between indulging his reckless behavior or trying to spend the day making a difference.

It's mostly there. I have included, or at least hinted at, the character arc, internal conflict, and intimate want, though it's a bit clunky and the theme feels too on the nose. Let me try one more pass:

> Arrogant weatherman Phil Connors is pissed about having to spend another Groundhog Day in Punxsutawney, PA. All he wants is for the day to end, but thanks to a cruel quirk of the fates, he is caught in an endless time loop, reliving the day over and over again. Living in a world with no consequences, Phil indulges his most twisted and reckless fantasies, but the excitement fades when he realizes there is no escape and he will forever be trapped in the temporal distortion.

As always, I could clean more and punch it up, but for the sake of a Story Pitch this is all I need!

10
USING YOUR STORY PITCH

BEFORE WE GET to using a Story Pitch for writing outlines, handling character issues, and writing your book blurb, let's focus on how it can be used as a recalibration tool. You can use a Story Pitch to get back on track after getting lost in your writing, and as a check-system before doing rewrites. The process for doing these is the same:

Steps for using a Story Pitch as a recalibration tool:

- 1) Reread your Story Pitch and compare it to your story.
- 2) Decide which direction is best: the direction of the Story Pitch or the direction of the story.
- 3A) If you decide both are blah, reexamine the story elements in your Story Pitch.
- 3B) If you decide the story is better, rewrite your Story Pitch to match it.
- 3C) If you decide your Story Pitch is better, then

check your manuscript for all the elements of story we've discussed.
- 3C-I) If elements are missing, then decide how to introduce them into your story.
- 3C-II) If elements are not missing but are different, then adjust your story to match the Story Pitch.

1) REREAD YOUR STORY PITCH AND COMPARE IT TO YOUR STORY.

Read the two and take note on where the elements of story diverge. Continue to step 2.

2) DECIDE WHICH DIRECTION IS BEST: THE DIRECTION OF THE STORY PITCH OR THE DIRECTION OF THE STORY.

This is generally a gut instinct situation, but if you're having trouble, ask yourself, "Why am I writing this story in the first place?" Try to pinpoint what it was about the story that excited you and decide which fits best: the story you wrote or the Story Pitch. Compare your answer with steps 3A, 3B, and 3C and continue to the matching step.

3A) IF YOU DECIDE BOTH ARE BLAH, REEXAMINE THE STORY ELEMENTS IN YOUR STORY PITCH.

There is a chance you made an error with your original Story Pitch and the story you tried to tell isn't as powerful as you meant it to be. If that happens reexamine the story elements from your Story Pitch. Without realizing it we sometimes make weaker choices in our writing. For example, you could have picked stakes that had high consequences, but failed to connect with the character or their wants. Take the time and analyze each element making sure each is strong. Once you've made the changes and are ready to reevaluate, begin again at step 1.

3B) IF YOU DECIDE THE STORY IS BETTER, REWRITE YOUR STORY PITCH TO MATCH IT.

It's okay to deviate from your Story Pitch. Execution rarely comes out exact and as a writer learns their characters and gives them voice, the characters sometimes decide to do what they want to do and not what the writer wants them to do. That's a good thing. And if your characters and plot have deviated, then simply extract the elements of story from what you've written and use them to rewrite your Story Pitch. Once you've made the changes and are ready to reevaluate, begin again at step 1.

3C) IF YOU DECIDE YOUR STORY PITCH IS BETTER, THEN CHECK YOUR MANUSCRIPT FOR ALL THE ELEMENTS OF STORY WE'VE DISCUSSED.

Write down the elements of story from your manuscript side by side with the ones you used to write your Story Pitch. Compare your answer with steps 3C-1 and 3C-2 and continue to the matching step.

3C-1) IF ELEMENTS ARE MISSING, THEN DECIDE HOW TO INTRODUCE THEM INTO YOUR STORY.

There is a chance that in writing you got distracted and forgot to introduce an element or that you had decided not to bother with a character arc or a theme. If that's the case, then figure out what is missing and make plans on how to reincorporate the missing elements into your story. Once you've made the changes and are ready to reevaluate, begin again at step 1.

3C-II) IF ELEMENTS ARE NOT MISSING, BUT ARE DIFFERENT, ADJUST YOUR STORY TO MATCH THE STORY PITCH.

Don't be scared of making a big change. Sometimes when pre-writing or when writing you can choose the wrong POV character or go with stakes that are too weak. When realizing the flaws, make the changes you need to make, even if they are hard to write. Always go with the stronger choice. Once you've made the changes and are ready to reevaluate, begin again at step 1.

RESIST THEM:

I'm about nine thousand words into *Resist Them* and it's a hot mess. Using the steps above, I'm going to try and figure out what's wrong.

STEP 1) REREAD YOUR STORY PITCH AND COMPARE IT TO YOUR STORY.

In my story, I have set up the POV character's life and wants, but there is no clear direction where things will evolve from there and it only slightly resembles my Story Pitch. I will proceed to Step 2.

STEP 2) DECIDE WHICH DIRECTION IS BEST: THE DIRECTION OF THE STORY PITCH OR THE DIRECTION OF THE STORY.

My Story Pitch is the story I want to be telling. I'm not happy with the partially written story. I will proceed to step 3C.

STEP 3C) IF YOU DECIDE YOUR STORY PITCH IS BETTER, THEN CHECK YOUR MANUSCRIPT FOR ALL THE ELEMENTS OF STORY WE'VE DISCUSSED.

In the story, I'm missing conflict from the part of the government. What I have on the page just seems off. I'm also not fully touching upon the themes I want to hit. While writing my Story Pitch, I decided that the big issue is Randdol doesn't go through a traditional character arc and that his world view is limited, so the readers aren't seeing everything they need to see. I will proceed to step 3C-I.

STEP 3C-I) IF ELEMENTS ARE MISSING, THEN DECIDE HOW TO INTRODUCE THEM INTO YOUR STORY.

To fix my story, I'm going to add a second POV character to *Resist Them*. Her name is Tayes. She will be a police officer working for the government and her life will juxtapose nicely with Randdol's to make it clear that there are two parts to this dystopian world.

11
FIXING CHARACTERS

ONE OF THE most powerful things about a Story Pitch is that you can write one for any important character in your story. If you're writing a story that has more than one POV character, I recommend writing a Story Pitch for each one. Doing an epic fantasy with six POV's? Then crank out six Story Pitches! Writing a romantic comedy with each love interest doing their own POV? Then write two Story Pitches! It's that simple and if the task of writing a Story Pitch for an additional POV character feels too daunting, then maybe you need to really ask yourself if the point of view is even worth having in your story.

The biggest hurdle I have to deal with when fixing *Resist Them* is creating a second POV character. Generally, you can't just do that on the fly, so in an attempt to get to know the second POV character better I'm writing a Story Pitch for them.

So here we go:

- POV Character - Tayes is a police officer working for the government.
- POV's Big Want - Wants to keep order in the city.
- Core Conflict - Needs to stop Randdol from trying to free himself and overthrow the government.
- The Stakes - If Tayes fails to stop Randdol, the whole government could crumble. If the government somehow survives, she will be punished for failing and will be exported out of the city.
- The Genre - Science Fiction, Dystopian, Thriller
- Voice - Dystopian world is extra dark and can broadcast directly into people's heads.
- Maine Theme - How a government controls, or doesn't control, its people.
- POV's Intimate Want - Wants to do her job without dealing with stupid work politics.
- POV's Character Arc - Starts as being not a fan of the system and government, is forced to question it, and then will decide either to re-embrace it or turn against it.
- POV's Internal Conflict - Torn on what is right, wrong, and best for the city.

If I spun all those things into a Story Pitch it would turn out something like this:

STORY PITCH

In a near future, where the government broadcasts directly into its citizen's mind, Commander Tayes's only want is to keep the city of Hata safe, but Randdol Mupt keeps getting in her way. Now armed with secrets he shouldn't possess, Randdol risks bringing down the entire government. Frustrated by work politics and a broken system, Tayes is forced to decide if she will stop Randdol or if she will help him bring down The Word.

From writing that I now know the story I want to tell with Tayes. I also know when I read it in conjunction with my original Story Pitch that her POV and Randdols will balance nicely. Plus, there will be major conflict and internal struggles between the two as they face off, adding a deeper layer to the story.

If you are writing a story that has multiple points of view, doing a Story Pitch for each of your main POV characters can help you plan out the structure of the story and make sure you're giving each character enough attention without shortchanging any of them.

A Story Pitch can also help you solve problems with non-POV characters. If you are having trouble connecting with the supporting cast, or can't seem to get into the head of your antagonist, then doing a Story Pitch for those characters can help.

All the characters in your story should have their own wants and life outside of the scenes where your main POV character is. The reader does not always need to know the exact details of these hidden lives, but bits and pieces should be visible. A story will not work if the supporting cast seems to only exist for the sake of your POV character. By doing a Story Pitch for each of these characters, you'll get a better understanding of their wants, what's getting in the way, and how their needs might cause conflict with your other characters.

12
OUTLINING

My favorite way to use a Story Pitch is for outlining. If you're using a standard three-act structure, then a Story Pitch will tell you the most important beats for your story.

Looking back at Resist Them's Story Pitch we have:

> In a near future, where the government broadcasts directly into its citizen's mind, Randdol Mupt is merely a man who wants to enjoy food that's not mush. Upon accidentally learning the truths that the government doesn't want its people to know, he chooses to resist. Now being hunted by an elite soldier, Randdol must free himself from enslavement or risk becoming a drone with no sense of self or memory of who he is.

From that Story Pitch we know that the structure must be something like:

- Randdol lives/exists in this dystopian world.
- Randdol wants to just enjoy food and the basic things in life.
- Randdol learns world is what it is.
- Randdol chooses to resist the government.
- The government fights back and sends an elite soldier after him.
- Randdol and the government face off... one or both lose.

That's the basic structure of the story I want to tell. We already talked about character arcs and how the three-act structure works. Using that as a basis I can simply add the missing scenes in between each of those core elements. Or if I was more of a "pantser" I could jump forward and start writing knowing at least where everything was heading.

If I were to break down and do another pass it might be something like this:

Randdol lives/exists in this dystopian world:

- Randdol living in a dark/gritty world
- Set up how bad and horrible this society is

Randdol wants to just enjoy food and the basic things in life:

- Randdol at work/with friends showing other side of his life
- Randdol at home showing him eating literal mush

Randdol learns world is what it is:

- Catalyst of some sort with Randdol starting to awaken from his ignorance
- Randdol testing or probing to make sense of new knowledge
- Randdol really accepting new knowledge

Randdol chooses to resist the government:

- Randdol forms a plan on how to fight back
- Randdol begins to enact plan (doesn't work)
- Randdol readjusts plan and enacts it

The government fights back and sends an elite soldier after him:

- The government learns of Randdol's plan
- The government fights back
- Cat and mouse game of Randdol and government trying to outsmart each other

Randdol and the government face off… one or both lose:

- Randdol and the government have big face-off
- Randdol and the government have mental face-off
- Randdol wins or loses

From there I could jump in and start writing, or if I

wanted a more fleshed out outline, I could break all those sections down even further. For example, I know that there will be a second POV character in Resist Them so let's see how I might handle that first section in more detail:

Randdol lives/exists in this dystopian world:

- Randdol living in a dark/gritty world.
- Randdol on the way home from work witnesses an assault.
- The evil/secret-police show up, scaring the crap out of Randdol.
- The victim of assault is arrested and Randdol is almost arrested, too.

Set up how bad and horrible this society is:

- Tayes (police officer) oversees the arrested person being brought in.
- Tayes work-life establishes a class system between Randdol and the citizens verses what the police and government's living conditions are like.
- Tayes meets with her boss to talk about recent crime spree.

If you like light outlines, then this should be enough to get you to start writing. But if you're the kind of person who still wants a more detailed outline, then continue from there, adding specific dialogue for scenes and notes about what conflict, plot points, or character reveals happen in them. If you like a more rigid or traditional Hollywood structure, then it would also be easy to mold your Story Pitch outline to fit that.

Another benefit of using a Story Pitch for outlining is that you can apply it to any size of story. Working on a three-thousand-word short story? Then all the techniques still work. Writing a novella or novel? They still work. Even crazier is that they can also be used for a series of books, too. I recently applied a Story Pitch to my epic fantasy series and instead of looking at just book one I looked at the arc I plan to tell for all nine books.

Applying a Story Pitch to such a large piece of work sounds intimidating, so let me do one for the Harry Potter series so you can see what it might look like:

- POV Character - Harry Potter, a boy wizard.
- POV's Big Want - To stop Voldemort.
- Core Conflict - Voldemort wants to destroy the magic & muggle worlds
- The Stakes - Beyond his own life, the lives of all his loved ones is on the line, as is the home he has made for himself in the magic community.
- The Genre - Contemporary Fantasy
- Voice - A whimsical story set in modern times focusing on kids going through a magical school system.
- Main Themes - Not fitting in, Good vs. Evil, Finding Self Confidence

- POV's Intimate Want - To find his place in the world.
- POV's Character Arc - Grows from not having a home and fitting in, to gaining a family and building a place he can call home.
- POV's Internal Conflict - Torn with self-doubt.

If I plug that info into our starter template it looks like this:

Harry Potter desperately wants to find a place where he fits in and after finally doing so at Hogwarts, Voldemort, a dark wizard, threatens not only to kill all those he loves, but to destroy the magic society.

And a rewritten fleshed out Story Pitch for the entire Harry Potter series could look like this:

Harry Potter, the boy who lived, never fit in with his extended muggle family and always knew something was missing from his life. After unlocking magical abilities, he finds a new home and family at Hogwarts, a school for witchcraft and wizardry. Finally feeling like he belongs, Harry's new life is put at risk when Voldemort, his parent's murderer, and a master of the dark arts, returns to take over the magical community and to destroy the boy he failed to kill.

Keep in mind that Harry is the POV character for the

series, so the Story Pitch is really about his arc from book one to where he ends at book seven, as well as Voldemort being the driving antagonistic force throughout the series. If I was struggling with the supporting cast I could easily rewrite the Story Pitch to focus on Ron, Hermione, or even Voldemort.

13
BLURBS

FUTURE-SCOTT, here (not to be confused with Future-Eric, or Future-Tom… long story). I am writing this section about blurbs three-and-a-half weeks after finishing the rest of this book. I'm writing from the future where I have also finished *Resist Them* and sent it to my editor. Armed with all my future-knowledge, I'm at a point where I'm ready to write the blurb!

A book blurb has a few meanings, but here's the one mostly used in the indie scene: A description of a book for use on the back cover, marketing, and sales sites like Amazon, Kobo, Nook, and Apple.

You already know that a Story Pitch is a writing tool that only the author sees. A blurb, on the other hand, is meant for marketing and will be read by lots of people. Because it's meant for gaining sales, blurbs must be approached differently. A blurb requires copywriting. This is a specific type of writing that is meant to influence those who read it into taking action (in our case, buying a book). My background is not in copywriting, so if you want an in-depth look at how to do it there are lots of great books on the subject. I'm only going to go into the basics here.

Book blurbs have a strict structure. They open with a hook to draw the reader in. Then there's a section that sets up the world, character, or story. Then the blurb ends with a call to action telling the reader that they should buy the book.

A simple way to understand this is to look at non-fiction blurbs, such as the one I have written for *Story Pitch*:

> Struggling to start your story or lost in the middle? You need a Story Pitch.
>
> A standard pitch is meant for marketing and selling, but a Story Pitch is a powerful tool meant to be used when pre-writing and writing. It can help you jumpstart your novel, screenplay, comic, or whatever type of story you are trying to tell, and it can be used as a corrective measure if you get off track during the writing process.
>
> In this book, you'll learn:
>
> - The key elements to story
>
> - How those elements are connected
>
> - How to construct a Story Pitch
>
> - How to use a Story Pitch for outlining
>
> - How to use a Story Pitch to fix character problems
>
> - How to use a Story Pitch when lost during writing
>
> - How to use a Story Pitch for writing book blurbs
>
> If you like honesty, no bull, a bunch of humor, and tons of examples in your writing guides, then you'll love Scott

King's *Story Pitch*. Buy *Story Pitch* today and start writing your story!

A non-fiction blurb is easy because non-fiction books are about solving a problem. Readers have something they need to know and the non-fiction book is saying, "Here is how you solve that thing that is causing you trouble!" That's why the blurb for Story Pitch starts right off with trying to make it clear which problems it answers. That's my hook. The second section is all the middle junk explaining what the book is. The end of the blurb is the call to action.

Sounds really simple, right? Hook. Middle junk. Call to action.

It's the middle junk where a lot of authors get lost and that's what's so great about your Story Pitch. It is the middle junk! Plus, the hook is most likely your voice element. That means to write your book's blurb all you need to do is deconstruct your Story Pitch and then make it all flow in a pretty way!

Let's look at *Resist Them*'s Story Pitch:

In a near future, where the government broadcasts directly into its citizen's mind, Randdol Mupt is merely a man who wants to enjoy food that's not mush. Upon accidentally learning the truths that the government doesn't want its people to know, he chooses to resist. Now being hunted by an elite soldier, Randdol must free himself from enslavement or risk becoming a drone with no sense of self or memory of who he is.

My hook is clearly the "In a near future, where the government broadcasts directly into…" It makes the genre clear and offers some mystery to make people want to know more. Adding a call to action at the bottom instantly makes my deconstructed Story Pitch look like a blurb.

> In a near future the government broadcasts directly into its citizen's mind!
>
> Randdol Mupt is merely a man who wants to enjoy food that's not mush. Upon accidentally learning the truths that the government doesn't want its people to know, he chooses to resist. Now being hunted by an elite soldier, Randdol must free himself from enslavement or risk becoming a drone with no sense of self or memory of who he is.
>
> Scott King's *Resist Them* is an action-packed adventure that fans of *1984* or *The Handmaid's Tale* will find unable to put down. Buy the book now and decide if you resist them.

Beyond the rough writing, there are two big problems I see here. The first is that there is too much information. I don't need to mention Randdol's intimate want. If it were somehow enticing or added a sense of mystery, like my hook, then I could keep it, but otherwise it's just extra information that's not needed. So, I need to trim out any part that's not reflecting the essence of the story I told.

The second issue I have is the lack of uniqueness. The sense of originality and voice that I establish in my hook doesn't show up again. The whole thing feels generic. Since the voice element that makes my story unique is the broadcast, I'm going to try and include that in the blurb.

After another pass, I end up with this:

In a near future the government broadcasts directly into its citizen's mind!

The Affirmation occurs twice a day, at 8:01 exactly. No matter what you are doing or where you are, it plays directly in your head. Day in and day out it repeats…

Resist Them. Trust The Word. The Word will not lie. It is loyal to you. It wants you great. It wants you safe from The Opposition. The Opposition wants to take. They want your freedom. They want your thoughts. They want you. The Opposition will come. When it does, resist them.

After learning the truths that the government doesn't want its people to know, Randdol Mupt is hunted by an elite soldier, Randdol must free himself from enslavement or risk becoming a drone with no sense of self or memory of who he is.

Scott King's *Resist Them* is an action-packed adventure that fans of *1984* or *The Handmaid's Tale* will find unable to put down. Buy the book now and decide if you resist them.

Overall, I like this structure much better. It gives a clear feel for what the story is. It's interesting without giving away spoilers. At this point, if a potential buyer reads this they should know the exact kind of story they're getting. As a blurb, it still doesn't work. The middle junk is too clunky and doesn't flow right. I need another pass at copywriting to make it a better read.

The thing to remember is that the blurb is not a summary of your story. It is a taste. A hint at which reader expectations will be met in the story. It's a tease where you let just enough information slip out, but hold back the rest to leave the reader wanting more.

In your finished story, you have lots of room to make a reader connect with your POV character. You have almost no chance to do that in a blurb. That means when selling your story, make sure you ramp up things like stakes, core conflict, or any powerful internal conflict that your POV character experiences. Hard choices and insurmountable situations work crazy well in book blurbs.

A rewrite to clean up my pitch would look more like:

A near future where the government broadcasts directly into your mind!

The Affirmation occurs twice a day, at 8:01 exactly. No matter what you are doing or where you are, it plays directly in your head. Day in and day out it repeats…

Resist Them. Trust The Word. The Word will not lie. It is loyal to you. It wants you great. It wants you safe from The Opposition. The Opposition wants to take. They want your freedom. They want your thoughts. They want you. The Opposition will come. When it does, resist them.

After decades of repeating The Affirmation, a botched surgery causes Randdol's beliefs to quiver, and he unravels the truth behind The Word. Now, while being hunted by an elite soldier, he has a choice to make. Will he join The Opposition or will he resist them?

Filled with twists, and high-octane action, Scott King's *Resist Them* is a dark dystopian thriller set in a future all too close to our own. Fans of *1984* and *A Brave New World* will revel in this fast-paced thrill read. Grab it now and decide which side to join!

For the hook, I dropped the "citizen's mind" and changed it to "your" to make it more personal. I want someone to read the hook and then ask themselves, "Oh god, what would happen if the government could broadcast right into my head?"

The middle junk is just enough of a tease to make people want to know more about the world. I also cut things like Randdol's intimate want, but overall you should be able to read the blurb and see the essence of my original Story Pitch as well as the elements of story that are hidden inside of it. It's clear what Randdol wants and what is getting in the way. The stakes could be a bit more emphasized, but the blurb was already getting long, and you want to keep it concise, plus I decided the choice of resisting or not was such a great hook that any extra word space should be dedicated to it.

Once you have a finished blurb, it's time to try it out on other people. It's not easy putting yourself out there. Sharing your blurb can make you feel vulnerable, but getting feedback is the only way to make sure your blurb is enticing.

Before taking feedback, consider how they physically reacted when they heard or read the blurb. Were they engaged? Did they look away or were their eyes glassy? Were they mostly paying attention, but then at a specific point shuffled in their seat? Did they cringe at a part where you wanted them to chuckle?

Upon hearing someone's feedback to your blurb, make sure you also know what kind of reader they are. Giving a clean romance reader the blurb for your horror sci-fi story won't give you the needed feedback. So, make sure that the person is objective enough to give good feedback or, even better, that they're the target audience you're trying to sell your story to.

Share your blurb with as many people as you can. Pay close attention to what they find intriguing. Figure out any parts of your pitch where they get bored and distracted and then take all your feedback and do another pass. Eventually your blurb will be sparkly and so influential it will suck in even the most skeptical reader.

STEPS FOR CONVERTING A STORY PITCH TO A BLURB:

- Pull out your voice element and make it your hook.
- Deconstruct your Story Pitch and rewrite to make your middle junk flow.
- Add a call to action to the bottom of the Story Pitch.
- Pull out any extra information from your Story Pitch that doesn't offer a hint of mystery.

- Make sure the genre and voice elements are still clear.
- Ramp up the conflicts and stakes to hold the reader's attention.
- Bust out your copywriting skills and clean the whole thing up.
- Share your blurb and tweak it till it's done.

14
WHAT NOW?

YOU WROTE A STORY PITCH! You should now have a clear mental image of the story you wish to tell. The next step is simple… you need to write it.

I'm all for education and expanding one's knowledge base to become a better writer, but at the end of the day if you want to be a writer, you must write. I talk about this a lot in *The 5 Day Novel* and, if you are looking to get into the right mindset and figure out the rhythm of your workflow process, it's worth checking out.

If you are someone who hates outlining, then use your Story Pitch and jump right into writing. If you are someone who must have a crazy detailed outline, then just use your Story Pitch to create one. The important thing here is that you get to the actual writing process.

Writing is not easy. Don't let anyone ever tell you that it is. It takes stubbornness and the willingness to make writing a priority in your life. Yet the benefits are amazing. Stories have the power to change the way people think and see the world. The question is… how badly do you want to make a change? How hard are you willing to work to leave your mark on the world?

I've been doing this for years. I've seen so many people start writing and never finish. Don't be one of those people. Don't begin on your journey and give it up, because the only thing that separates those who want to write from those who write is making the time to put words on the page.

I have faith in you. I think that if you want it bad enough, you will make writing a part of your life. No one else can make you a writer. Only you can do it. So ask yourself, how bad do you want it?

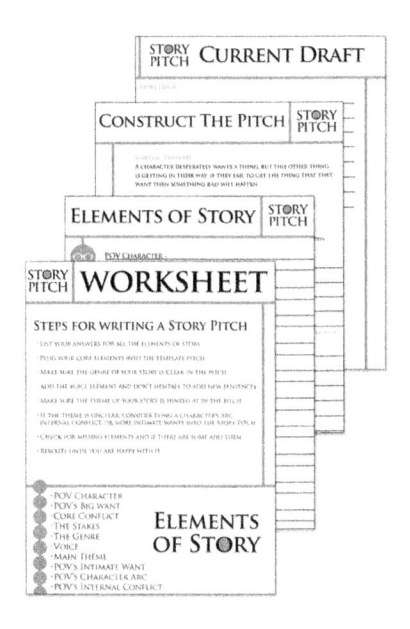

Struggling to construct your Story Pitch? Join Scott's mailing list and get free access to a PDF worksheet that you can print out and use!

Get the worksheet here:

http://www.scottking.info/blog/story-pitch-worksheet/

Note to the Reader

Thank you for reading *Story Pitch*. If you enjoyed the book, I hope you'll consider leaving a review. They're the lifeblood of indie authors and the most important factor for other readers in deciding if they will pick it up.

ABOUT THE AUTHOR

Scott King is a writer, photographer, and educator. He was born in Washington, D.C. and raised in Ocean City, Maryland. He received his undergraduate degree in film from Towson University, and his M.F.A. in film from American University.

Until moving to Texas to follow his wife's career, King worked as a college professor teaching photography, digital arts, and writing-related classes. He now works full-time as a game photographer and author.

As a board game photographer, King shoots games for websites, online stores, and for other marketing needs. He also produces an annual calendar that highlights board and other hobby games.

To learn more about Scott and his work, visit his website at www.ScottKing.info. You can also follow him on Twitter via @ScottKing.